Searching for Authenticity

John Offutt

Dedicated to Carla

My best friend…my partner…my wife

Searching for Authenticity

Confronting Issues Every Church
Needs to Face

John Offutt

Searching for Authenticity

Confronting Issues Every Church Needs to Face

ISBN-13: 978-1721943975
ISBN-10: 1721943978

TABLE OF CONTENTS

INTRODUCTION

I am on a quest! I am searching for something so significant that it has the potential to change whole cultures and nations. This search is not mine alone. It is taking place all around the world. We are looking for people who have embraced the message of Christianity and have become true disciples of Jesus.

The Pew Research Center reports there are 2.3 billion Christians in the world, so such a search should be brief. True disciples should be commonplace within American Christianity. But they are not. As Christian scholar, Dallas Willard wrote, "For at least several decades the churches of the Western world have not made discipleship a condition of being a Christian."

It is tragic how easy it is to find those who profess to have a relationship with Jesus but fail to model His character to those outside the church. This core contradiction is summed up in a story I read a few years ago:

"A man was being tailgated by a stressed-out woman on a busy boulevard. Suddenly the light turned yellow, just in front of him. He did the right thing, stopping at the crosswalk, even though he could have beaten the red light by accelerating. The tailgating woman was furious and honked her horn, screaming in frustration as she missed her chance to get through the intersection, dropping her cell phone and makeup.

As she was mid-rant, she heard a tap on her window and looked up into the stern face of a state trooper. He ordered her to exit her car with her hands up. He then took her to the station where she was searched, fingerprinted, photographed and placed in a holding cell. After a couple of hours, she was escorted back to the booking desk where the arresting trooper was waiting with her personal effects.

He said, "I'm very sorry for this mistake. You see, I pulled up behind your car while you were blowing your horn, flipping off the guy in front of you, and cussing at him. I noticed the 'What Would Jesus Do?' bumper sticker, the 'Choose Life' license plate holder, the 'Follow Me to Sunday School' bumper sticker, and the chrome-plated Christian fish on the car. Naturally, I assumed you had stolen it."

It is easy to chuckle at this story, partly because of how we can identify to the truth of it. At times we have been the guy in the lead car, and sadly many times we've been the infuriated woman driver. The story exposes the problem within the ranks of Christianity today. For many who identify themselves as Christians, there is a gap between what we say we believe and the lives we live. How many times we have heard unchurched people say, "I don't attend church because there are too many hypocrites!" That word is defined as "one whose actions belie stated beliefs." This disparity haunts the effectiveness of Christianity throughout our culture. It also serves as the motivation for my search.

A life of authenticity is not about religious creeds or denominational affiliation. It is about an honest representation of the attitudes, values, and actions of Jesus in our personal lives.

I have been in pastoral church ministry since 1974. Throughout my years of experience with Christians, I have seen first-hand how the culture has distracted many well-meaning believers from living a spiritually authentic life. The impact of this inconsistency among believers is a weakened, less effective corporate church.

During my ministry, I have been encouraged to put my observations and experiences in book form. I hesitated because I didn't want my writings to be viewed as another "cheap shot" at the church. Many already criticize the global church as a relic that should make way for a more relevant expression of Christianity. However, for all its faults, the church is still God's instrument for change.

I knew I could not address the issues covered in this book as theory or biblical perspective. I wanted to make sure I had personally experienced everything I chose to write about. The experiences and observations I've cited are both positive and negative. They have not made me an expert on life, church or ministry. However, they have taught me valuable lessons about God's desire for us to authentically represent His character.

This book's subtitle is "Confronting Issues Every Church Needs to Face." Why would I bring the church into the discussion of authenticity? Because I hope this book will spark some honest evaluation of what is happening within our churches.

When I refer to the church in this book, I am not referring to any denomination, organization or institution commonly associated with the word *church*. I am talking about an expression of Christianity that emerges when people come together in a corporate setting to express their faith. The church corporately is only a reflection of the individuals within it.

Christians cannot live in isolation. We cannot think of the church as an independent entity to which we share no personal responsibility. It is not an organization to which we belong or a building in which we worship. It is a group of followers of Jesus Christ. If the issues discussed in this book are ever to influence the function of the church as we know it, change must first occur within the hearts of people who constitute the church.

I hope this book will challenge the status-quo stagnation that characterizes the spiritual experience of many Christians. I want to rekindle passion in believers who have grown complacent in their Christian experience. Imagine what could happen if the individuals of the church became passionate followers of Jesus. Imagine how the church could influence the darkness of our culture. Imagine how the church could expand the Kingdom of God!

Please join me in this quest.

John Offutt
John Offutt Ministries
Lindale, Texas

Chapter 1

LIMITATIONS OF TRADITION

Little men with little minds and little imaginations go through life in little ruts, smugly resisting all the changes which would jar their little worlds.

Zig Ziglar

I first encountered the crippling power of tradition in church life when I became pastor of a small church in the early 1990s. Up until then, all my pastoral experience consisted of serving in associate staff positions in larger churches.

My expectations for this congregation proved to be so naïve. This church had a reputation for being a "pastor killer," but I didn't know it before I took the position. It only took a few months for the controlling element of the congregation to begin opposing the direction I felt the church should go.

I thought all a pastor had to do was show clearly what

the Scripture says about a subject, and people would accept it as true and adjust accordingly. I know, I told you I was naïve. Soon my pastor bubble burst, and I had to endure a harsh reality that troubles me to this day. I realized when many church people are faced with a choice between what Scripture teaches and the experience of their tradition, Scripture is seen as irrelevant.

About a year into our ministry, things reached a boiling point. The church had already changed in many ways. We made a transition of worship style, church government was adjusted to reflect our changed direction, and a second service was added to keep up with our growth.

None of these changes pleased the dissenting element. About 85 people banded together to plan an exodus from the church. I don't like people being upset, so I attempted to reconcile the situation. I scheduled a meeting with the group, thinking I could fix things. Did I mention I was naïve? Before going into the meeting, I felt the Lord tell me not to defend myself because the conflict was not about me but about His plans for the church. For two hours, I sat in silence as I was verbally assaulted in every way imaginable.

The longer I sat in silence (as I felt the Lord had instructed), the angrier the group became. I soon realized they had not come to reconcile, but to fight. After the longest two hours of my life, one of the older men in the church said, "If I ask you a question, will you at least answer it." I said I would, and I braced myself for whatever was coming next. He asked, "Just what do you think the

2

role of a deacon is in the church"? I immediately went to Acts 6 and began to explain what the Scripture stated. But before I could finish, he interrupted me and said, "We know what the Bible says about it. We want to know what you say."

Even in a meeting that hostile, I still wasn't prepared for such a response. Suddenly, the core issue of the conflict became crystal clear. They viewed scripture as subservient to tradition. The 85 left that meeting, and most never returned to our church. Over the next several years God grew the church to several hundred people who impacted the community in many ways. I believe this growth happened because when we were at the crossroad of choosing either God's leadership or tradition, we chose to follow God regardless of the cost.

When I talk about tradition, I am referring to human-inspired methodologies of ministry, not biblically based practices that form foundations of our faith. One issue I have with the modern church movement is that key directives such as baptism, discipleship, fasting, prayer, giving, sexual purity, etc. are being considered disposable "traditions." The church is doing an injustice to the younger generation by not teaching them to appreciate and practice these Christian foundations. By contrast, liturgical churches (Catholic, Orthodox and Protestant ones with a set order of services) have for centuries held fast to traditions on all manner of religious practices.

Traditions developed by men (even godly men) have

3

often been elevated to reverence even beyond that of Scripture. This is not a new dilemma; Jesus told the Pharisees "...you have invalidated the word of God for the sake of your traditions," He went on to say, "This people honors Me with their lips, but their heart is far away from Me. But in vain do they worship Me, teaching as doctrines the precepts of men" (Matthew 15:6-9). When we allow our traditions to dictate our communion with God, we nullify the power of our worship of God.

Does this mean the church can never change? No. Through the centuries God has introduced many new things to build up His church. These include new hymns and worship songs, new instruments of worship, new translations of Scripture, new methods of evangelism (TV, radio, films), new ministries to address specific needs (marriage, addiction, youth, stewardship), even new mission approaches to reach specific cultural and religious groups.

One of the most challenging things for people in the church to do is cultivate an environment of honest and objective evaluation so they can change. It continues to amaze me that so many Christians act as though God never changes the way He operates from generation to generation. True spiritual vitality is maintained when there is a freedom to ask hard questions about the effectiveness of what we are doing.

Several years ago, our church faced one of those painful evaluation moments. We had developed a small group ministry that was thriving. At the same time, our Sunday school was withering. We tried everything we could think of to revive it. We renamed it, restructured it, added new materials and personnel. All attempts to revitalize it were failing. Though the Bible doesn't say every church needs a Sunday school, tradition has made it seem so.

We came to a painful conclusion: if a ministry is dying despite all efforts to revive it, while another is thriving, we must be willing to let the dying ministry die. This is easy to say or write, but so hard to do.

Our tradition has trained us to believe whatever gets started must be maintained. That is why there are shells of once-effective ministries still being propped up long after their life has gone. Why do we find it so hard to put our energies into that which God is currently doing? There is only one answer—our tradition.

Albert Einstein once said, "We can't solve problems by using the same kind of thinking we used when we created them." His words echoed the wisdom of Jesus when he answered a question posed by His disciples.

"But no one puts a patch of unshrunk cloth on an old garment; for the patch pulls away from the garment and a worse tear results. Nor do people put new wine into old wineskins; otherwise the wineskins burst and the wine pours out, and the wineskins are ruined, but they put new wine into fresh wineskins, and both are preserved" (Matthew 9:16-17).

How does this teaching relate to tradition? Jesus uses two visual illustrations to make His point about holding onto old things and missing new works of God. A well-worn garment may make for comfortable clothing but is not a picture of healthy Christianity. I have an old sweatshirt like that. It is stretched out, discolored, and yes ugly, but so comfortable to wear. Of course, my wife Carla will not let me wear it out of the house. Why? It is no longer presentable. Some of our ways, comfortable though they may be are no longer presentable for reaching the culture around us. A new garment is required. It doesn't mean the old one was never any good. Did you notice Jesus said a worse tear results when we refuse to replace the garment? There are things worse than change. The worst is missing what God wants us to do.

The wineskin illustration makes the same point. When the fresh wine was made, it could not be placed into old wineskins because the stretched-out leather could no longer expand during fermentation. If new wine were poured in, the old wineskin would break because of its rigidity. Jesus instructs us to "place new wine into fresh wineskins."

How many times have we lost new and fresh opportunities with God because we tried to force them into old ways, forms, structures, methods, etc.? I believe one of the obstacles to accepting the fresh moves of God is <u>fear</u>. That's right, we are afraid to accept the possibility that God wants to lead us and His church (not ours) into new experiences and direction. But, isn't it worth the risk if the reward is to drink the new wine of God's Spirit and His calling in our lives?

Facing our fear of man

It didn't take long for me as a young pastor to come face to face with fear! Not fear associated with Satan, our spiritual adversary. I'm talking about fear of the people in the pews.

Our church was growing at an explosive rate. New people were coming, but by the same yoke, many had left the church. I was surprised each week to see the faces of people who decided to return. God was transforming lives, and people from various denominational backgrounds were calling our church their spiritual home. As the diversity increased, so did the expressions of worship.

People began to raise their hands, clap or speak out during worship as they expressed love and adoration for the Lord. This was something never seen before in this church, and as you can imagine, some religious members were uncomfortable with it. I did not understand then, but I now know that religious people are typically uncomfortable with free expressions of love and obedience before God.

As the weeks went by, so did the complaints about "those people." Don't you just love that label? I had become good friends with several of these new members of our church family who expressed worship by raising their hands. I knew their motives were pure. But, in an ill-conceived effort to make peace in the church, I wrote each of them a letter trying to explain the transition of our church, the misunderstanding of their freedom and some other spiritual-sounding comments. And they did exactly what I asked them to do. They stopped their outward expressions of worship.

But, that's not all that stopped. Before writing the letter, our services were filled with passion each week, families were being restored, and people were dedicating their lives to following Jesus. After I sent the letter, you could ice skate down our center aisle. You've been in those services, haven't you? Everyone keeps looking at their watch and praying for it to end.

This went on for three weeks and then God, and I had a conversation. One day, I heard God speak as clearly as if He was right in front of me. He asked, "Are you going to run this church or are you going to let Me run it? If you are, I will let you, but if you want Me to run it, then get out of the way!" Wow, that was a life-altering moment for me. It put my fear of displeasing people in a proper perspective.

I immediately called each person I had written the letter to and asked them to forget that they ever received it. I said they were free to express themselves as God led them. The following week the passion of our church service returned. God is not confined to the ways that He has worked in times past. He is looking for believers and churches in every generation that will take the risk to follow Him and accept the freshness that He wants us to experience.

God has always operated in this way. He looks at a need and responds in ways relevant to what the situation required. As God declared through the prophet Isaiah, "Do not call to mind the former things, or ponder things of the past. Behold, I will do something new; Will you not be aware of it? (Isaiah. 43:18-19a)

Sadly, many believers will not be aware of what God is doing because they refuse to accept the possibility that something new is even necessary. Consider the arrogance of that mindset. We as the created telling the Creator we don't think anything new is needed. Do we really want to take that position? Oh, I know we are more subtle and religious sounding than that, but that is what we are saying. God has revealed His heart to us; He wants to show us new things, remove our reliance on past ways and experience His freshness. And we dare to say, thanks, but no thanks!

It seems that "change" is a dirty word for many Christians. We are afraid of it; we try to avoid it; we develop excuses why we can't do it, and we vilify anyone who attempts to bring it about. Let's not kid ourselves, change is difficult, but change is inevitable!

When I met with the search committee of the church, that I mentioned earlier, I asked about their feelings regarding change. They assured me they knew the church had to change to remain viable. We discussed in detail what changes were needed. Again, there was agreement between every person on the committee. They, like most people, view change as a great idea until it starts to happen.

I recently attended a congregational meeting of a church desiring to relocate to another area in their city. Now, that is a huge change. The church leadership wanted to move to an area experiencing new growth of young families.

I could feel the tensions rise as people expressed differing viewpoints. In this kind of meeting true feelings are exposed, and the inconsistencies in the arguments against change are revealed. I heard many good points, but then an elderly gentleman expressed what many others were thinking. He said a move like that would be too much for him, and if the church approved the relocation, he would have to leave his church of many years and go elsewhere.

Does the irony and inconsistency of that statement grip you? I know he was sincere, and I fully understand his choice was painful. By his own admission, whether he moved with the church or went to another church, he would not be attending church at the same place. Change was going to happen in his life one way or the other.

We as church leaders must accept some of the responsibility for this type of reaction. In our zeal to move the church forward, we may be too quick to discount the contributions of those who have gone before us. I know I have been guilty of that type of decision making. In my desire to be fresh and innovative, I dismissed all previous methodology and swung the pendulum too far.

The role of a leader is taking the people with you on the

journey. It is good to be a visionary, but you can't get so far in front of the people in the congregation that they lose sight of where you are going. This usually opens the door to resistance and distrust If we are not very careful, we as church leaders can become reactionary in our leadership. When this occurs, we become part of the problem in the church, not part of the solution.

This reality has tested my patience more than once. At times I quickly recognized it, and other times I missed all the signals of the true condition of the church. A pastor's challenge is to honor the heritage of the church without being held hostage by it. The modern church needs to be reminded that God works in new ways in every generation. The question is how do we bridge that divide?

There are basically four phases that a church goes through when its life and passion are replaced with traditionalism. I have heard these four phases described as the movement, the monument, the museum and the mausoleum. Let's look at them individually and see how the process affects the typical church.

Phase One: The Movement

A movement begins when an outpouring of God's presence leads people to action. They are no longer satisfied with the status quo in their life, their church, and their culture. A movement transforms the rhetoric of the church into experience.

A spiritual movement is characterized by people being

11

willing to take a risk with God. These people see the needs of the world differently than most people. They see God as being sufficient for all things. They see His calling for them is to be personally involved as part of the solution to those needs.

Most churches get started as part of a movement. There is vitality, passion, purpose, and mission. There is nothing more empowering and fulfilling than to be part of something you know is an extension of God's activity on the earth. It is during these movements that God's kingdom expands, and the culture is influenced for righteousness.

Phase Two: The Monument

As a movement grows, some always arise who insist there must be more structure for it to sustain its growth and effectiveness. This usually results in building bigger church buildings and adding layers of organization and personnel that were not part of the initial movement.

Now, I am not saying these things are wrong. I have done my share of monument building. The problem is that a monument shifts our focus to a place rather than an experiential spiritual lifestyle. What do we do with monuments? We observe them, we visit them, we honor them, and we view them as a reminder of something not related to current church life.

The evidence of this is confirmed by the history of the early church. After the birth of the church in Acts 2, it expanded rapidly. This expansion happened with no technology, no seminaries, no bookstores, no church buildings and no trained clergy. Matter of fact, being a Christian or proclaiming the gospel message was against the law in many places. It was truly a movement.

In 313 AD it all changed with the Edict of Milan when the Roman Emperor Constantine he made Christianity the recognized religion, built church buildings and provided professional clergy to operate the church. The result was astonishing. It hindered church growth rather than increasing it. How could that be? It took the day-to-day lifestyle out of Christianity and moved it into something separate from daily life. Therein lies the danger for Christians in our culture. We can go down this subtle path with a sincere heart without realizing we are draining the life-giving power out of church life.

Now, don't misunderstand me. The church does need some organization and structure, but only enough to facilitate ministry. When the structure controls the direction of life-sustaining ministry, we have drifted from a movement and have become a monument.

Phase Three: The Museum

The world's great museums display priceless antiquities which are viewed and appreciated by millions of visitors each year. These antiquities are what they appear to be—relics of a past era you can see but not touch. This is not the kind description we want to be applied to the Christian life and the church of Jesus.

The museum stage occurs when our emphasis becomes about what God used to do rather than what He is currently doing or wants to do in the future. It is just like viewing the museum relics. They look beautiful, but we can't utilize them in modern life.

Sadly, that is the condition of many churches in our culture. These congregations become curators of great memories. They love to hear messages and sing songs about a God who now seems too distant to be relevant in our present church life. These once spiritually engaged people now see their role as the protector of the relics in the museum.

When a church begins to put more emphasis on safeguarding things of the past than God's current activity, they are becoming a spiritual museum. This stage also surfaces when people in churches attempt to recapture or recreate the feelings of the "good old days" by doing what was done then. This may bring nostalgia, but it is an ineffective model for Kingdom ministry.

Phase Four: The Mausoleum

Throughout my years of church ministry, I have participated in more funerals than I would like to remember. After most funeral services there is a procession of family and friends to the cemetery for the burial. Most cemeteries offer the family a choice of a grave or an above-ground burial structure called a mausoleum. Some mausoleums are simple and basic, while others are large and elegantly decorated. However, all mausoleums have one thing in common: they contain no life, only death. It reminds me of the conflict Jesus had with the religious establishment represented by the Pharisees. They had become a mausoleum, and Jesus told them so:

"Woe to you, scribes and Pharisees, hypocrites! For you clean the outside of the cup and of the dish, but inside they are full of robbery and self-indulgence. You blind Pharisee, first clean the inside of the cup and of the dish, so that the outside of it may become clean also. Woe scribes and Pharisees, hypocrites! For you are like whitewashed tombs which on the outside appear beautiful but inside they are full of dead men's bones and all uncleanness. So you, outwardly appear righteous to men, but inwardly are full of hypocrisy and lawlessness" (Matthew 23:25-28).

Everything looked good on the outside, but there was no spiritual life in them. The worst thing about their condition was they did not even recognize their own lifelessness. That's what God was saying to the church at Laodicea in Revelation chapter 3. They were lukewarm, naked, and blind but they saw themselves as the opposite of what God saw. They had been lulled into the belief that all was okay.

One of the saddest accounts in scripture is the downfall of Samson. Judges 16 shows him as a man who took his spiritual commitment lightly. After he revealed the source of his strength to the temptress Delilah, she again

15

summoned the Philistines to seize him. Samson said, "I will go out as at other times and shake myself free." He did not know the Spirit of the Lord had departed him.

Wow, what a startling reality for us in the church. Is it possible to go about our religious activity and not even realize God's Spirit has left us? I believe the answer is YES! Services are still held, songs are sung, sermons are delivered, activities are scheduled, and offerings are received, but God's Spirit is no longer present.

So, what do we do? How do we get a picture of what "biblical normal" looks like? I think the place to start is in the Book of Acts. In the early church, new believers allowed their faith to move them beyond boundaries of their religious traditions. Faith motivated these Jewish believers to embrace God in ways far different from anything they had experienced.

After the Day of Pentecost in Acts 2, the new believers began to come together for teaching, prayer, fellowship, and communion. Their love and passion for God had a dramatic effect on the way they conducted themselves toward others. In their lives we see a compelling portrait of what an authentic body of believers can look like:

> *We see a church where…concern for others out-weighs concern for self.*

> *We see a church where…sacrificial generosity is a normal expression.*

We see a church where...community is a priority.

We see a church where...relationships flourish outside the church.

We see a church where...the gospel produces life transformation.

We see a church where...spiritual freedom exists.

We see a church where...Christ-followers are committed to spiritual growth.

We see a church where...signs and wonders are common experiences.

We see a church where...those in the culture are attracted to the gospel.

We see a church where...people are added to the Kingdom daily.

Those of us in the current Christian culture may dismiss these early church experiences as "the way God moved in previous generations." For the sake of our traditions, we convince ourselves to wait for someone else to be the voice that introduces a new era of authentic Christian experience.

But, what would happen if we stopped dismissing these possibilities and began to imagine what our church could be? Could church life be like that again? That question has led me to other questions that I encourage us all to contemplate. Why can't it be our experience? Why not us? Why not now?

Personal Inventory

Answer each question based on what is true today in your life. This will point out places you need to adjust your perspective and experience. If unsure, answer what is predominantly true.

1. I agree God operates differently from one generation to another.

2. I actively look for areas where God is currently working.

3. I do not rely on my past experiences to determine my view of the church.

4. I am willing to adapt to change when necessary.

5. I focus on what God is doing now rather than depending on the past.

6. I support honest ministry evaluation and the hard decisions that may be required.

7. I am more concerned about obeying scripture than maintaining any tradition.

8. I will embrace risk (the unknown) for the benefit of the Kingdom of God.

9. I accept new ideas even at the expense of the way things have been.

10. I allow God the freedom to do what He desires without restraint.

Count the number of "yes" answers and number of "no" answers. If you have more "no" answers than "yes" answers, you need to re-evaluate your view of tradition as it relates to your church experience.

Chapter 2

EMBRACE OF
INSTITUTIONALISM

"The church has an unnatural love affair with organization."

David Wilkerson

We Americans love organization. So much so that companies have created many products to satisfy this desire. We can buy organizers for our closets, kitchen, desk, garage, office and other things. We can purchase phone apps to organize our busy lives. We can visit stores that specialize in selling the best organizational containers for storage. We can even hire an "organization specialist" to come into our home or office and do the work for us. Our culture seems obsessed with a desire for organization.

As with all cultural influences, this obsession has invaded the church. Many well-meaning Christians believe

21

the church must embrace a business model of organization. We have adapted structural and organizational principles from the world and are attempting to squeeze spiritual ministry into that mold.

That approach to ministry is flawed from the beginning. The world's kingdom and God's kingdom operate in sharp contrast to one another. Many churches have become so organized that it is difficult to accomplish anything of eternal significance. They have placed their focus on the mechanism of ministry rather than ministry itself.

The ministry machine pressures pastors to keep all the plates spinning – to preach, counsel, do weddings, funerals, hospital visits, social events, finances, manage the master calendar and meet other expectations of those who attend. Have I ever been frustrated about it? Have I ever complained Yes!

But, if I may speak as a life-long church leader to church leaders, much of this is our fault. We have created the ministry machine, so we must keep it running. I like the way Charles Swindoll describes this problem in his book, *Dropping Your Guard*: "Many churches are like that impressive invention which had hundreds of wheels, coils, gears, pulleys, bells, and lights which all went around and rang and flashed at the touch of a button. When the inventor was asked about the function of the weird machine, he replied; What does it do? Oh, it doesn't do anything, but doesn't it run beautifully."

Now, I can already hear the arguments for organization and structure; I have heard them all before. I have been in leadership meetings where spiritually minded leaders divided the church into two sections: the spiritual and the business. They said, "Though this is a church, we must manage it as a business because we have assets, property, liabilities, and budgets."

Yes, the church needs to operate with integrity and accountability. But let's set something straight from the beginning. There are not two sides to a church (ministry and business). There is only one side, and it is ministry. Once a church views itself as part business, the business mentality soon overshadows the ministry. It sets the church on a path to institutionalism.

This is a hard concept for church deacons, elders, administrators, committees and boards to accept. Our culture and their professional experience have convinced them that church business must be managed by the business model. This has led to more church conflicts than I have time to describe. Each time a conflict erupts over organization and structure, I am reminded of what a stronghold this has become in the church.

Some of the most confrontational meetings I have ever been involved with were regarding business management, structure, and organization of the church. One could argue these battles were all about authority, control or power within the church, but that would not be a sufficiently accurate conclusion. These conflicts are an expression of the philosophy of the world that has invaded the church.

This philosophy became strikingly evident at a church I had been pastoring for five years. Our leadership team consisted of all staff pastors and elders. For months we discussed business and organizational structures that our elders desired to implement. After coming to an impasse, I thought we needed to shift the discussion back to its biblical basis so we could regain clarity. I spent several days preparing a four-page document which turned out to be a simple written version of my personal ministry philosophy on structure and organization, developed over 40 years of ministry experience.

This philosophy had guided our ministry throughout my tenure. So, there wasn't anything revolutionary about the content of the document I had prepared. My philosophy is simple, and I believe it is the way the early church operated. *"Effective ministry dictates the need for structure; structure should not dictate ministry and does not ensure effective ministry."*

These elders were my friends; they were men who served side by side with me; they were men who had pledged to love and support one another. You can imagine my shock when they said, "We disagree with everything in this document."

What? Are you kidding me? How is that even possible? It is possible because many good people in the church have been deceived into believing there is a business side of ministry that must be handled in a business-like way. Sadly, that difference in philosophy caused a conflict we could not resolve. Within a year, my ministry within that congregation came to an end.

I believe the warning Paul gave to the Colossians is applicable to us in the church today: "See to it that no one takes you captive through philosophy and empty deception, according to the tradition of men, according to the elementary principles of the world, rather than according to Christ" (Colossians. 2:8).

When I use the word institutionalism, my definition is: "an organization or establishment used for promoting a cause or program." Institutionalism well describes the church's efforts to perpetuate itself.

Jesus did not come to give birth to an institution, but to an organism. A living organism is *"a life form that consists of mutually independent parts, functioning together."* It is a life source, filled with passion and desire to operate in freedom. Every church regardless of size has an organism within it; even if it is being restrained by the organization or institution. The very nature of an organization or institution is to focus on systems, operational procedures, controls, conformity, and regulations.

By contrast, the early church reflects the function of an organism. "They were continually devoting themselves to the apostles teaching and to fellowship, to the breaking of bread and to prayer. Everyone kept feeling a sense of awe;

25

and many wonders and signs were taking place through the apostles." (Acts 2:42-43)

After Constantine legalized Christianity in 313 AD, he made professionals of the pastors and placed the gathering of the church into buildings. That was the beginning of the institutional church. The organism that had operated freely and changed the known-world became the servant of the institution.

Here are some subtle characteristics to look for when a church begins changing from an organism to an institution:

- People become viewed as assets to be managed, rather than individuals who need to be led and loved.

- Being a Spirit-generated and Spirit-empowered disciple of Jesus is not as important as membership.

- Resources are viewed as fuel to maintain and strengthen the organization, rather than a channel to reach the local community and the nations.

- Worship ceases to be a lifestyle of encounters with God and is relegated to a set schedule of morning and evening services.

- Relationships are valued based on adherence to church standards; they are viewed as an

26

acceptable casualty for those who do not conform.

- Priorities become whatever is necessary to keep the organization functioning.

- Church involvement takes precedence over the pursuit of righteousness, love, grace, and maturity.

- Evangelism changes from a member's intentional witness of the gospel to inviting people to hear a person preach a sermon.

- Pastors and staff are viewed as employees who require management, rather than as spiritual leaders, called by God and placed in the church to be honored and followed.

- Leadership is modified from Spirit-filled passion and ministry gifts that serve people to an organizational flowchart with titles and positions.

- Ministry success is measured by the number of people who attend services rather than the life transformation of those who attend.

- Conformity to the organization becomes the requirement for unity.

Can we honestly say the church as we know it has not drifted from being a living organism into an institution? This subtle process has inverted the church's message of the Christian life so much that church involvement is viewed as equivalent to a Christ-imitating lifestyle.

Now, this does not mean the church is promoting things which are evil or wrong. It just indicates the church has drifted from its original intent. The focus has been slowly distracted to the matters of form over function, thus diminishing the effectiveness of the church. An institutional practice of church cannot fulfill the mission of the church. Therein is the source of the dilemma for many churches and their leaders. As a church leader, I have hit my head up against the institutional wall many, many times. These experiences have made me keenly aware of how institutionalism shows up in the lives of those in the church. Here are some examples:

1. Ministry adaptability is replaced with ministry gridlock

The early church had a unique ministry ability that has been displaced in the modern church. It could adapt quickly to the needs of people. In Acts 2:44-45 and Acts 4:32-35, the church took immediate action to distribute resources to their fellow believers who were in need. In Acts 6:1-4, the church selected the first deacons to serve the practical needs of the people, thus enabling the Apostles to focus on the priorities of ministry. In Acts 13:2-3, the church sent out the first missionaries from

28

within their group. In Acts 15, the church settled its own dispute regarding the gospel being presented to the Gentiles. These few examples show they had a ministry mindset rather than an institutional one.

In contrast, how quickly can the modern church discover a need, evaluate it, determine the solution and meet the need? Let's be honest; the time is usually not measured in hours or days, but by weeks. The church has developed such a layered structure that it is impossible to adapt quickly to changing situations. If the early church recognized the pace of situational change, how much more should we remember it in the 21st Century? Today's world is so fast-paced that our rigid church structures have become a weight tied around our neck. The typical church requires so much time to decide on a matter that when a decision is finally made, the situation has changed from when the decision-making process began.

Another influence in the institutional church is our American ideal of democratic government. The church is not a democracy. It is a movement of people whose lives are submitted to Jesus as Lord. The world's political structure is one of gaining power, exercising control, developing agendas, aligning support, and catering to select constituents. The Jesus model of leadership expressed so well in Philippians 2:5-8, is quite the opposite: "... although He existed in the form of God, did not regard equality with God a thing to be grasped, but emptied Himself, taking the form of a bond-servant, and being made in the likeness of men. Being found in appearance as a man, He humbled Himself by becoming obedient to the point of death, even death on a cross."

We see the results of our government philosophy play out before us in the news every day. Our country's political parties have drawn lines so deep, progress cannot be achieved on anything. Our political system is in gridlock. When the church adopts this same structural mentality, the same result occurs. The democratic system should feel biblically unnatural for people submitted to the King of Kings.

The government-like structure of the modern church most often divides people. There must be a winner and loser; the side with the most support or votes wins. There is no motivation to gain consensus within the church. It becomes much more about human agendas and posturing than it does about following God's will.

2. Spiritual warfare is replaced with institutional maintenance

Anyone who has served in the church understands the reality of spiritual warfare connected to ministry. It comes with the territory. Jesus said to his disciples, "Behold, I send you out as sheep in the midst of wolves; so be shrewd as serpents and innocent as doves." (Matthew 10:16)

He also said, "If the world hates you, you know that it has hated Me before it hated you. If you were of the world, the world would love its own; but because you are not of the world, but I chose you out of the world, because of this the world hates you" (John 15:18-19).

Wow! Who wouldn't want to sign up for that ministry assignment? But wait, we did sign up for it! Every church leader knows ministry is a struggle between the kingdom of darkness and the kingdom of Light. The church is designed to be a mighty army that the gates of Hell cannot withstand. Jesus intended the church to be moving forward and conquering territory from the kingdom of darkness.

As the church, has become more institutional, we have lost that spirit and become more passive and rigid. The focus is no longer on what we can conquer, but on what we can protect and manage.

This reality is confirmed by a survey of pastors conducted by World Vision and published in the book, *The Hole in the Gospel,* by Richard Stearns. The survey asked pastors to rank the priorities for their churches. The results:

79%.... worship

57%.... evangelism

55%.... children's ministry

47%.... discipleship programs

18% …. helping the poor and disadvantaged

The results illustrate how we have made the ministry of the church "about us" rather than about the world outside the church building. In the book, *Radical*, by David Platt, he tells of a Christian publication which had two headlines side by side. The one on the left said, "First Baptist Church Celebrates New $23 Million Building." The article described in vivid detail the church's new sanctuary with its exquisite marble, intricate design and beautiful stained glass. The smaller article on the right read, "Baptist Relief Helps Sudanese Refugees." The article described how 350,000 refugees in Western Sudan were dying of malnutrition and without aid might not live until the end of the year. The last sentence said that Baptists had sent money to help relieve their suffering. David said he was excited until he read the final sentence. Remember, the article on the left celebrated the dedication of a $23 million building. The amount sent to Sudan was $5,000. The contrast is staggering: Millions spent on an institutional monument and just $5,000 for hundreds of thousands of starving men, women, and children, most of whom were dying without Christ.

This type of disparity in church priorities is evident in churches of all sizes. After the 2010 earthquake in Haiti which devastated the capital of Port-au-Prince and surrounding area, the world mobilized to help thousands of the homeless. In the church I was pastoring at the time, many felt compelled to help in any way possible. A group of women led a relief project that raised $10,000. The church also committed to building three homes for families who had lost everything in the earthquake.

Since the recovery was so long and the conditions remained so grave, another fund-raising project was planned to provide food and medicine to the children in the affected area. By then the attitude within the church had changed. There was outspoken resentment about sending money to Haiti rather than using it for our own church. After much debate and discord, a decision was made to use the money they raised to buy play equipment for the children of our church, to help fund musicians for the church and for some other church-related desires. How could the daily survival of children in a devastated country be compared to providing a playground for church kids? Honestly, it shouldn't be. But this type of distortion often occurs in the modern church.

One of the harshest warnings of Jesus concerns the coming judgments and is in Matthew 25:31-46. He describes how he will welcome into his eternal kingdom those who have fed the hungry, given drink to the thirsty, clothed the naked, cared for the sick, visited the prisoners and welcomed strangers. He goes on to say he will banish to the fires of Hell those who haven't done these things.

Our acts of love, generosity, kindness, compassion, hospitality, and prayer are plundering the kingdom of darkness. When our focus becomes inward, the offensive power of the church is diminished.

I believe the more people embrace an institutional mindset, the more conflicts arise. It is still spiritual warfare, but the points of contention are often so trivial. Most of us have experienced church conflicts over matters with no eternal significance. Is it worth fighting over what shade of green the nursery is painted, what kinds of flowers are planted out front, where the church buys its toilet paper, or that the youth pastor never wears a tie? Sadly, it does, and this list could be endless.

3. Ministry vision is replaced with programs

One of the most important things for a church to possess is a clear vision of its purpose. Proverbs 29: 18 reads, "Where there is no vision, the people are unrestrained." When the church knows where it is going, it helps us get priorities right and keep the main thing, the main thing.

However, church vision is not a "one size fits all" reality. This has been complicated in our ministry culture where vision can be marketed like any other product. Church leaders sometimes buy into the idea that a growth plan which was successful for one church will produce the same results in their church. The problem with this mindset is that vision is church specific. It is about the church's dreams of what could be.

Many church leaders have succumbed to the pressure of adding an "action-packed" church calendar of programs as a substitute for true vision. How many take the next step and ask "why" the calendar is full and "why" a certain program or activity exists? People who love the institutional church may even consider such questioning insubordinate.

But, if we are going to refocus, we must have the courage to ask, "Why?"

During objective evaluation, I have found that things we thought were part of our vision existed for our own benefit and pleasure. The church needs to part with the myth that it can be all things to all people. If that objective continues to be the motivation for the church, the focus will only become more inward. This self- perpetuating influence has bound the church to its buildings, programs, and activities.

The two things that matter most

In the Great Commandment, Jesus stated a spiritual truth which should be a foundational principle for the church. During a discussion with the Sadducees and Pharisees, one of them asked Jesus, "Teacher, which is the greatest commandment?" He answered, "You shall love the Lord your God with all your heart, and with all your soul and with all your mind."

Having a God focus is top priority, but there is more to Jesus' answer. He goes on to say, "The second is like it, you shall love your neighbor as yourself" (Matthew 22:36-39).

That changes the whole perspective. It is no longer about just me and God. It now includes the needs of others. This truth has posed an interesting question for Christians in every generation. The question that continues to demand an answer is, "Who is my neighbor?"

In Luke 10: 25-29, a lawyer asked Jesus, "What must I

do to inherit eternal life?" Jesus answered with a question of His own, "What is written in the Law? How does it read to you?" The lawyer replied, "You shall love the Lord your God with all your heart, and with all your soul, and with all your strength, and with all your mind; and your neighbor as yourself." Jesus said he had answered correctly, but to justify himself, the man asked, "And who is my neighbor?"

Isn't it interesting how we so often struggle with putting the needs of others (neighbors) on an equal plane with our own? The lawyer wasn't concerned about loving God, but the issue of loving his neighbor tripped him up. Aren't we still asking the same question? By our actions, aren't we narrowing our list of who we see as our neighbor?

Jesus answered "the neighbor question" by sharing a parable now known as the Good Samaritan in Luke 10:30-37. I love this parable because it shows the futility of religion and the power of grace. The lawyer who Jesus answered was well trained in Jewish law. So Jesus used in his story a priest and a Levite, both of whom avoided the man in need.

Then Jesus did the unthinkable. He used a Samaritan, a group considered half-breed infidels by the Jews, to make His point. But when he (the Samaritan) saw the injured Jew, he had compassion and came to his rescue. At the end of the parable, Jesus asked the lawyer, "Which of these three do you think proved to be neighbor to the man?" Can you imagine? The man who had been taught to despise Samaritans his whole life had to answer, "The one who had mercy on him." Then Jesus gave the command that has echoed throughout church history, "Go and do the same."

Since the words of Jesus are so clear, why do we continue to struggle to get outside the walls of our church buildings? Richard Stearns says, "If church leaders do not have an outward vision to become salt and light in our world, to promote social and spiritual transformation, pursue justice, and proclaim the whole gospel, then the church will fail to realize its potential as an agent of change. It will become inwardly focused on meeting the needs of its members, to the exclusion of its non-members. It will be a spiritual cocoon, where Christians can retreat from a hostile world, rather than a 'transformation station' whose primary objective is to change the world. We need only to read our church bulletin to see where our priorities have been placed. How many of the announcements involve programs that focus more on meeting our needs than the needs of those outside the church?"

Stearns continues, "When our churches become spiritual spas in which we retreat from the world, our salt loses its saltiness, and we are no longer able to impact our culture." Morgan Chilulu, an African pastor of a small church ministering amid the AIDS pandemic said, "A church that lives within its walls is no church at all." He is right.

The church's shift toward institutionalism has left us seeing the vision and practice of the early church as a distant dream of idealistic people. Many within the church no longer see it as a pattern we can practically follow. This shift is well described in Rubel Shelly's book, *I Knew Jesus Before He Was a Christian – and I Liked Him Better Then*.

"With the imprint left by Constantine...the church lost its identity as an organism and became an organization. It lost its virtue as the corporate expression of Christ and turned into a religious corporation. The church abandoned its calling to be a microcosm of the kingdom reign of God for the sake of becoming a location, an event to witness, a political force, or an entity whose favor could be courted by the world. Church gradually ceased being countercultural and became the dominant culture."

The early church experienced the wondrous works of God because they lived according to the pattern of Jesus. In a world that is starving for authenticity, people are not looking for another institution; they are looking for the reality and simplicity of Jesus. We in the church have the answer, but adjustments are necessary if we are to display a real picture of the Kingdom of God.

Is it possible God looks upon our embrace of institutional church with the same disdain that Jesus expressed to the Pharisees? God's disgust with religious forms and practices pierces like a dagger in two prophetic messages from the Old Testament. Though they were written thousands of years ago, they sound like God just spoke them yesterday.

"Quit your worship charades. I can't stand your trivial religious games; monthly conferences, weekly Sabbaths, special meetings—meetings, meetings, meetings—I can't stand one more! Meetings for this, meetings for that. I hate them! You've worn me out! I'm sick of your religion, religion, religion, while you go on sinning. When you put on your next prayer-performance, I'll be looking the other way...Clean up your act. Sweep your lives clean of your evildoings, so I don't have to look at them any longer. Say no to wrong. Learn to do good. Work for justice. Help the down-and-out. Stand up for the homeless. Go to bat for the defenseless" (Isaiah 1:13-17 MSG)

When I look back over my years of ministry, I sometimes become angry. My anger is not directed at any one person or group of people. Most of the time, it is directed at myself for the role I have played in the distortion of the church. I can identify with the world's confusion about the gap between what the church says and what it does.

The way Jesus did ministry

One of my favorite authors, Gordon McDonald, wrote an article in *Leadership Journal* entitled, "Strange Things, Strange People, and Strange Places: The Unorthodox Ministry of Jesus." In it, he suggested that "the way Jesus made his ministry happen might not be acceptable among many orthodox and conservative organizations today." At the end of the article, He shares six observations about Jesus' ministry style. It is a style embraced by churches seeking to function as an organism, but not so much in institutional churches.

39

Jesus spent the first thirty years of his life simply growing in stature and in favor with God and man. Immanuel (God among us) built bridges of understanding with family, neighbors, and fellow-Israelites before launching his rescue mission among them. He patiently enhanced his credibility with people as his own personality, character, and faith were molded by the Father. Part of my challenge as a pastor is to build bridges and to win credibility among people who dislike church people. Some have been so mistreated they find it difficult to believe any of us have a non-judgmental, non-mercenary agenda.

Second, the focus of Jesus' ministry was building people. He would often shun big crowds to spend time on a few ordinary people Are we too obsessed with building big churches, big ministries, and big names for ourselves? Do we ever give the impression those are our driving motives? Jesus cares about people, and people have names and life situations that are complex. I want to learn to love people as He did. I believe God will bring the healing we need in Christ-centered communities of love. Those supportive communities are what the New Testament calls churches.

Third, He refused to entangle himself in institutional activities. Yes, Jesus went to the temple and synagogue, but he spent most of his time teaching at parties, on boats, in fields and walking along the road. In stark contrast to people then and now who measure success by size, numbers, and dollars, he was content to seek and confer significance by being ordinary, unnoticed, and humble. Your church doesn't need to battle for institutional and parachurch approval. The only authority we need to pursue is the kind Jesus had—the "moral authority" that comes from having integrity before the Lord.

Fourth, Jesus was big on denouncing injustice and self-righteousness but spent precious little time debating theology. He censured those who tried to set themselves up as judges of others' spirituality, but he was not inclined to condemn those who were at least traveling in the same direction as him. That is the point of the episode described in Mark 9:38-41. People don't have to be "one of us"—a member of your denomination or one who sees things the way you see them—to be known by Christ and blessed by him.

Fifth, Jesus always seemed more concerned about people's hearts than their heads. He was compassionate with women who had been immoral and men who were corrupt. But he was angriest when dealing with religious leaders and power brokers. Nobody can love the weak, pursue the powerless, and treat disreputable people with kindness without being suspect in a religious culture. What a tragic irony!

Sixth, the ultimate foundation for his ministry was his intimate relationship with the Heavenly Father. He drew strength from his Father's words. He withdrew from crowds to spend time in prayer. And the Father affirmed him by blessing what he did. For every hour of public teaching, there were many hours more spent in prayer, in small group training, and in compassionate ministry to wounded people.

This pattern of Jesus' ministry is the desire of almost every pastor I know. But sadly, the Jesus model is not the standard of measure when discussing the effectiveness of the modern institutional church. We should be assessing the success of our discipleship, our community outreach; and our releasing (and support) of people into parachurch ministry, church planting or missions. Instead, we look at membership numbers, finances, programs and facilities as measures of progress. This gives outsiders a blurred picture of Jesus.

The challenge for all pastors is to keep developing strategies to get Christians outside the walls of a building so the world can experience the authenticity of the gospel. Thankfully, many churches are breaking free of the institutional mindset and finding new ways to love their neighbors.

A good example of this happened in one church I pastored. A staff member began mobilizing the congregation for community service projects. We kick-started it with a "Compassion Week" designed to be an expression of love and commitment to those in the community. "Compassion teams" were formed so our people could choose their preferred area of service. Many families worked as teams so the parents could demonstrate to their children the importance of serving others.

Their group projects aimed at expressing the love of Jesus in simple yet practical ways. These included distributing bottles of water at the community ball fields, giving away quarters at a car wash, providing free hot dogs and drinks at the grocery store, doing yard work for seniors, and taking prayer walks in designated neighborhoods. It was gratifying to see how the community responded. At first, they were skeptical and wanted to know the catch. After they realized there wasn't a catch, they expressed great appreciation and openness.

We received letters and cards from neighbors expressing how our efforts had touched their lives. New people came to our church, saying it was because they had not seen a church do so many things so freely in the community before. Of course, the most significant impact was in the lives of the people who served.

In the First Century, a charge was brought against Christians stating, the church was "turning the world upside down" (Acts 17:6). Wouldn't it be great if the modern church could be described like that? The good news is it can be. But doing so will require us to break the grip of our institutional mindset. We break free by exercising faith, taking risks, and following God in absolute obedience. The reward will be a life-giving passion for God that enables us to function as the living organism the church was meant to be.

Personal Inventory

Answer each question based on what is true today in your life. This will point out places you need to adjust your perspective and experience. If unsure, answer what is predominantly true.

1. I agree the church is a spiritual organism; not a business.

2. I believe structure is only established to facilitate ministry.

3. I agree that structure does not ensure ministry effectiveness.

4. I believe the needs of people should take priority over the organizational structure.

5. I am personally involved in Kingdom activity.

6. I do not rely on church programs to accomplish ministry goals.

7. I am flexible and quick to adjust.

8. I am actively supportive of church leadership.

9. I believe the church's most effective ministry occurs outside the walls of the building.

10. I agree that the church should not be governed by a "political style" structure.

Count the number of "yes" answers and number of "no" answers. If you have more "no" answers than "yes" answers, you need to re-evaluate your view of institutionalism as it relates to your church experience.

Chapter 3

DISTORTION OF EVANGELISM

All those "in Christ" are commissioned to model and to declare, to experience and to offer the newness of life that is the kingdom of God."

Rubel Shelly

I was finalizing details for our worship service one Saturday evening when the phone rang. It was a man in our church who I considered a friend. He asked if he and another church member could come by my house and talk. I have learned through the years that calls like this on a Saturday night are rarely about casual conversation. As my two friends entered my home office, they said they had been circulating a petition among our church members.

That is something no pastor wants to hear, especially on a Saturday night. Petitions are never the best way to communicate concerns. They are divisive by nature, and I have never seen one produce a positive outcome in a church.

They wanted to change the style of my messages. They were questioning my commitment to evangelism because most of my sermons were expositional and focused on spiritual transformation. Unlike many evangelical churches in our area, I was not doing a salvation appeal each time I spoke. I understood this mindset. From the time I was a teenager, almost every sermon in every service was evangelistic. That did not make sense to me then, and it makes less sense to me now. I do not understand why people who are already Christians want to be told weekly how to become a Christian.

I tried to explain my ministry philosophy and my commitment to teaching the Scriptures. I was told, "People in our church require a different type of message." What? Have we come to the place when sermons are expected to be based on what people think they require? How does that leave room for hearing what God requires? Of course, I knew exactly what they meant. They were saying, give us evangelistic sermons and stop talking about so much about life transformation. I promised to pray about their concerns, but I knew I couldn't accede to this demand.

How has this mindset spread so far within the church? I believe that we, as leaders and members of the modern church have accepted and perpetuated a flawed view of evangelism without realizing it. The early church experienced explosive growth because the gospel was the fabric of their daily lives. The pattern of this growth is described in Acts 2:46-47.

"Day by day continuing with one mind in the temple, and breaking bread from house to house, they were taking their meals together with gladness and sincerity of heart, praising God and having favor with all the people. And the Lord was adding to their number day by day those who were being saved."

The early church's style of evangelism was effective because it was "naturally supernatural." New believers took their faith seriously and modeled it freely before people who had not yet believed. The result was people were receiving the gospel message daily. There is no New Testament mention of Sunday altar calls. Believers didn't expect pastors and elders to do most of the church's evangelism.

Before we can discuss the flaws in the way we present the gospel, we need to understand it. The word simply means "good news." It is the good news of a loving God, sending a sinless Savior to redeem and forgive hopeless and sinful people. I not only believe in the truth of the gospel but also in the power of this truth to produce salvation in even the most hardened heart. The Apostle Paul said, "For I am not ashamed of the gospel, for it is the power of God for salvation to everyone who believes…." (Romans 1:16).

Any person who receives this message, who seeks forgiveness of their sin, and asks Jesus to be their Savior and Lord will experience transformation that is soon evident. As Paul writes in 2 Corinthians 5:17, Therefore, if anyone is in Christ, he is a new creature; the old things passed away; behold, new things have come.

I identify myself as an Evangelical Christian (until I can find a better description). I have seen hundreds of lives transformed by the gospel. But I also have seen Christians turn off people who desperately need the gospel. They often speak of what we're against (abortion, same-sex relationships, restrictions of school prayer, etc.) and not much about what we are for. Others who identify themselves as Christians live no differently than those in the world. As a result, people who need our God look elsewhere for the answers. This should be alarming to us in the church.

The modern church must be willing to look deep into its belief system and identify the real reasons the world is rejecting the gospel message. Protectors of the status quo will say, "The gospel is being rejected because 'the god of this world is blinding people to the truth.'" They quote Paul's words in 2 Corinthians 4:3-4: "And even if our gospel is veiled, it is veiled to those who are perishing, in whose case the god of this world has blinded the minds of the unbelieving so that they might not see the light of the gospel of the glory of Christ, who is the image of God."

This is biblically true, but it is too easy to excuse ourselves from any personal responsibility for the church's condition. Don't you think the "god of this world" opposed the gospel in the church in Acts 2? Yet, even amid great opposition, the church flourished.

We, in the American church, can gain valuable insights by observing where the church has grown since the year 2000. The largest churches in the world are located outside the United States. The underground church movement in communist countries is multiplying at an unprecedented rate. Every year we hear reports of Muslims converting to Christianity all around the world.

Meanwhile, the American church is showing signs of decline and loss of influence. Why? It isn't because the "god of this world" is more powerful in the United States than he is in the rest of the world. In fact, most countries experiencing supernatural renewal are not politically free.

I am grateful for our freedoms in America, and I appreciate every man and woman who has fought to preserve those freedoms. However, we need to acknowledge that patriotism is not a synonym for godliness. Some have argued that the American church is diminishing because some of our liberties are being removed. While I too decry the loss of our civil liberties, we have to dump this flimsy excuse. We, in no way, face the same danger and opposition to Christianity as our brothers and sisters in other countries. They, like the church described in Acts 2, have grown without the benefit of religious liberty. Why?

If the struggle of the Western church is not about increased spiritual warfare or government opposition, what is it? Could it be that we are struggling because we have adopted a flawed view of the gospel? I believe God wants us to look at the gospel, evangelism, and salvation in a new light. Before you conclude that I am going down the slippery slope of heresy, let's examine what I think are the serious and dangerous flaws in the way the modern church views evangelism.

1. *Presenting the gospel as entirely heaven focused.*

Most evangelism training teaches its students techniques proven to engage a person in a discussion about their spiritual condition. It usually begins with this question, "Do you know where you will go when you die?" Or "Would you like to know how you can be sure you are going to heaven?" There is nothing biblically wrong with such questions. The issue of eternity is essential for all human beings. God created man with a living soul. But, is the gospel only for assuring entry to heaven after a person dies?

I believe the emphasis on heaven takes our eyes off the gospel's power to change us here on earth. It seems most American Christians are living under a depressive cloud. They feel life is hard; there is little hope, and the only way God can finally make it better is when we die and go to heaven. Who is attracted to that kind of gospel? It has given permission for Christians to live a victimized life and miss the power the gospel was meant to release. If heaven is the only reason to receive the gospel, then God should take us out of this life as soon as we receive it. Heaven is a great reward or benefit of the gospel. But, it shouldn't be the primary motivation to receive Christ.

The gospel is about restored relationship. One of the wondrous realities in the Garden of Eden was the relationship God and Adam enjoyed. The beautiful garden was a perfect showplace of God's creation. Adam and God would walk together there each evening. Can you imagine that? God enjoyed a personal relationship with the man He had created. That is what Adam and Eve lost when they sinned through the deception of the serpent and their choice of disobedience.

The Bible is God's description of His desire and commitment to restoring the relationship with mankind that was lost in the garden through sin. It is safe to conclude the gospel has more to do with a person's relationship with God than just life after death. Heaven is the eternal continuation of man's relationship with God that is restored when a person receives the gospel.

Paul goes on to say that when we have been reconciled to God, the Lord commissions us to proclaim the message of reconciliation. "...He has committed to us the word (message) of reconciliation. Therefore, we are ambassadors for Christ, as though God were making an appeal through us; we beg you on behalf of Christ, be reconciled to God." (2 Corinthians 5:19b-20).

How many Christians are missing the reality of restored relationships because they only focus on the heavenly reward of their salvation? One of the most significant benefits of being reconciled with God is the hope it gives us for others. It makes us want to bring this good news to our family, friends, and the world. The world is bleeding from countless broken relationships. What joy there is in helping broken people reconcile with God and with one another.

2. Evangelism is performed as an activity.

In 1978, I took a ministry staff position at a church near Dallas, Texas. I found it so different from my home church in Kentucky. Not only was it larger, but it was also more performance oriented than anything I had experienced. Church staff was held to a high level of accountability for the results we produced. Each week in a staff meeting we were expected to turn in a written report of the previous week's results. The form charted the number of home visits, number of gospel presentations, number of people who prayed to receive Christ, and documentation of the time spent performing each category. The expectation for each staff member was 15-20 hours of "visitation" or "witnessing" activity each week as well as the responsibilities of our assigned areas of ministry. The pressure to produce quantifiable results was relentless.

This church had a successful bus ministry that brought in hundreds of children each Sunday morning. The pressure was not limited to getting these kids to ride the bus to church. We had to be sure most of them also prayed to receive Jesus. If that occurred, it validated our work as effective evangelism.

I learned quickly, the more evangelism activities I could

perform, the more valued I would be as a staff member. We developed "soul-winning" programs to facilitate sharing of the gospel. These included door-to-door visitation, witnessing campaigns, street ministry, and many other activities. We would load 15 teenagers in a van and release them on unsuspecting people on street corners waiting for the stop light to change. We were gospel guerilla fighters. We also took teenagers to Daytona Beach to do evangelism with the college students who were there for spring break.

I know people have had a genuine salvation experience because of these programs. However, this type of ministry mentality has contributed to the compartmentalized thinking that is damaging to the church.

When evangelism is performed as an activity, it places emphasis on "what we do" rather than "who we are." Biblical evangelism is always an extension of the spiritual transformation that is seen in the life of a Christian. The conflict between "doing" and "being" is at the core of the flawed view of evangelism.

After Jesus arose from the grave, He presented Himself to the disciples and others over a period of 40 days. Just before He ascended back to His Father in heaven, He said to them:

"But you will receive power when the Holy Spirit has come upon you, and you will be My witnesses both in Jerusalem and in all Judea and Samaria and even to the remotest part of the earth." (Acts 1:8)

The words Jesus uses indicates something very personal. He said, "You will be" giving witness to your experiences with the Savior. He could have said "you will do witnessing" which is the way most Christians emphasize it. But giving witness of Christ's reality is more than "doing." It is about "being." It is about "who we are."

When the church accepts and promotes evangelism as an activity, it creates a salvation expressway filled with shortcuts aimed at getting the desired result. We push to get someone to say a salvation prayer rather than taking time to build a relationship and present a clear biblical explanation of the gospel leading to the conviction of sin and desire for forgiveness. A concern with numbers can also give birth to a "gunslinger" mentality, to see how many notches we can carve on our gospel gun. Thus it becomes more about our performance, than the spiritual needs of the people we evangelize.

This is a clear and present danger for the modern church. It is also why we are losing the battle of attractiveness with the world. In many churches, the gospel we are modeling is not appealing. We must always remind ourselves that we will give an account to God for the way we represent the gospel of Jesus.

3. Salvation measured by external criteria.

Many within the church have a false sense of security regarding their salvation experience. If you ask most professing Christians why they believe they have received salvation, the responses are quite similar. Usually, you will get an answer such as, "I asked Jesus to come into my heart 40 years ago," or, "I walked the aisle at a revival when I was 13." Others will say, "I raised my hand during Children's Church" or "I prayed a prayer with my teacher in Vacation Bible School." The similarities are obvious. Each response is based on an external act.

These all may be sincere commitments to Christ, but praying a prayer or responding to an altar call is not the biblical guarantee of salvation. Those things give no evidence of what has occurred in the person's heart.

I am concerned that we pastors are presenting a gospel requiring an action (raising a hand, praying a prayer, filling out a card, etc.) but it is void of repentance. We need to ask ourselves, "Can a person experience salvation without repentance?"

I have taught about repentance for many years. Early on, I defined it as "a change of direction, to turn around." I didn't realize it then, but I was promoting the idea that repentance is a "change of behavior." That is biblically incorrect. The Greek word for repentance is *metanoia*. It is a compound word; the prefix is *"meta"* which means "to change." The main part of the word is *noia* which means "mind or understanding." So, the actual meaning of the word is "to change one's mind." Therefore, the definition of repentance is "to change your mind or to believe differently."

This is what occurs in the hearts of a people when the Holy Spirit convicts them of their sin, reveals their need for salvation, and the individuals respond by repenting and committing their lives to Jesus. Repentance is an essential part of the gospel message. It was not just proclaimed by John the Baptist; Jesus also preached repentance. He said, "I have not come to call the righteous but sinners to repentance." (Luke 5:32).

When Paul stood before King Agrippa and proclaimed the gospel through his personal testimony, he declared the need for repentance. "So, King Agrippa, I did not prove disobedient to the heavenly vision, but kept declaring ... throughout all the region of Judea and even to the Gentiles, that they should repent and turn to God, performing deeds appropriate to repentance" (Acts 26:19-20).

These *"deeds appropriate to repentance"* are not things we must do to earn salvation. Paul made that clear when he wrote: "For by grace you have been saved through faith; and that not of yourselves, it is the gift of God; not as a result of works, so that no one may boast" (Ephesians 2:8-9). The deeds of which he speaks are actions that demonstrate a change in belief and direction. All biblical examples of repentance show such change. The works prompted by a changed heart do not save us from sin, but they give evidence that salvation has occurred. Look at the encounter between Jesus and Zacchaeus in Luke 19:1-10. He repented and received Jesus. The evidence of salvation is that he gave half his goods to the poor and restored fivefold that which he had stolen through his tax collecting business. There is no biblical example of people receiving the gospel who did not exhibit a drastic change in their character. This reality of change is what exposes the modern church's view of salvation and the gospel. We have communicated a gospel that requires no evidence of heart transformation.

The lack of change in a one who claims to be saved is a direct contradiction of the gospel itself. Just think about that for a moment. How can a finite human being encounter the God of the universe, receive Jesus into his life, become the dwelling place of the Holy Spirit and move forward in life with no noticeable change? That makes no practical sense, much less biblical sense.

As this mindset has permeated church culture, there has also been a corresponding increase in the use of the so-called "backsliding" label (which we will address in Chapter 4). A "backslider" may return to the altar for forgiveness many times. This is a natural and inevitable conclusion when we proclaim a gospel that requires no repentance and no outward change. The great danger in this is that we have convinced unconverted people they are safe.

Jesus always told the crowds that pursued him about the costs of receiving the gospel. He never made it easy or invited people to travel the wide road. He said becoming a true follower would require denying yourself and taking up the cross:

So then, you will know them by their fruits. Not everyone who says to Me, Lord, Lord, will enter the kingdom of heaven, but the one who does the will of My father who is in heaven will enter." (Matthew 7:20-21)

Does this mean all Christians reach a place of sinless perfection? No, We can and do fall in our spiritual walk. However, there is a vast difference between a transformed believer making a sinful choice and a person who has prayed a prayer, walked down an aisle, or filled out a church salvation card, but never demonstrated any evidence of a life change.

4. Presenting the gospel as the sole responsibility of the church.

When members of our church signed the petition, which stated their discontent with my preaching style, they were exposing a deeper church mindset on evangelism. That view is so unbiblical and damaging it has weakened the modern church and made it seem almost irrelevant to our culture. Their view is that Jesus commissioned the church to preach the gospel, thus making it the official duty of the institutional church. The truth is Jesus commissioned the *ecclesia*, which means "a called-out assembly." Every Christian regardless of nationality, race, creed, religious background or denominational affiliation is part of this "called out assembly." That means the responsibility and stewardship of the gospel are not given to an organization but to a living and breathing organism, the called-out assembly. Like those petitioners, many want to make

59

evangelism the job of the church and release individual members from personal responsibility.

This mindset is so insidious that it is rarely spoken; only written in petitions or spoken in whispers. They believe it is the pastor's job to preach salvation messages because the church pays his salary and he works for them. They consider the pastor their spiritual hireling or token substitute who removes them from any personal responsibility for evangelism.

Another level of deception of this mindset is exposed in the church when criticism arises that the pastor is a "teacher" and not a "preacher." This statement drives me nuts! Not only is it demeaning to the gift the Holy Spirit has placed within the pastor's life, but it is also unbiblical. Ephesians 4:11 lists the distinctive roles of apostles, prophets, evangelists individually but not pastors and teachers. Why? Because the service of a pastor includes teaching.

In many modern churches, pastors take on another role – as Christian entertainers. The people in the pews have become critics in the same way movies are critiqued by professional movie watchers. It's almost like we give points for delivery, excitement, oratory skill and other criteria. A church service and the pastor are judged on the member's scale of personal satisfaction.

A new pastor I met told me about the congregational vote approving his hiring. He said some who voted against him mentioned later they voted without having heard him preach. They said if they had heard him speak, they would have voted in favor.

I am not critical of the pastor. I have been in that position myself, and it is an awkward and vulnerable place. But the conversation revealed a core problem in our modern churches. The average pastor is judged by an external criterion based on performance. We should know by now that oratory doesn't ensure ministry effectiveness. If we are to measure a pastor's success, it should be by the spiritual health and maturity of the congregation and their responsiveness to sound teaching. The church has become quite good at critiquing sermons, but bad in the application of their contents.

Jesus said, "You are the light of the world. A city set on a hill cannot be hidden; nor does anyone light a lamp and put it under a basket, but on the lampstand, and it gives light to all who are in the house. Let your light shine before men in such a way that they may see your good works, and glorify your father who is in heaven." (Matthew 5:14-16)

The responsibility for presenting the gospel is that of every Christian regardless of where their paycheck comes from. It is more than a message; it is a lifestyle that we model. That is the biblical method of evangelism Jesus taught in the Sermon on the Mount. His light shining through us will attract others.

Our darkened culture needs to see the light and power of the gospel. Most of us are concerned because "taking the Lord's name in vain" (using a swear word with God's name attached) has become so commonplace in our culture. I believe the concern should be even broader. The word translated "take" comes from the Hebrew word *nasa*, which means "to carry or bear." The proper translation is, "Do not carry the name of the Lord your God in vain."

This encompasses a much larger application in today's culture. Those who profess Christ, who pray in His name, who take His name as a part of their identity, but who deliberately disobey His commands, are taking His name in vain. Because of the greatness of the name of God, any use of it that brings dishonor on Him or His character is taking His name in vain. The name of the Lord is holy as He is holy. The name of the Lord is a representation of His glory, His majesty, and supreme deity. We are to honor His name in our everyday lives. To do any less is taking His name in vain.

Rubel Shelly gives a classic summary of the church's responsibility for evangelism: "The church stands as a witness to the larger culture about what is possible for those who have not yet repented of their self-directed lives in order to believe the good news that God's kingdom rule is yet possible. All those 'in Christ' are commissioned to model and to declare, to experience and to offer the newness of life that is the kingdom of God."

Personal Inventory

Answer each question based on what is true today in your life. This will point out places you need to adjust your perspective and experience. If unsure, answer what is predominantly true.

1. I believe evangelism is a lifestyle rather than an activity.

2. I agree that the gospel is more about a relationship with God than it is about going to heaven when you die.

3. I accept that I am responsible for proclaiming the gospel.

4. I believe that repentance is necessary for salvation.

5. I agree there is more to evangelism than getting someone to repeat a prayer.

6. I have experienced "life-change" as the result of accepting the gospel.

7. I agree that evangelism is not just the pastor's responsibility in a sermon.

8. I believe a transformed life is the most effective form of evangelism.

9. I accept my role in performing the ministry of the church.

10. I accept my personal responsibility to be a "minister of reconciliation."

Count the number of "yes" answers and number of "no" answers. If you have more "no" answers than "yes" answers, you need to re-evaluate your view of evangelism as it relates to your church experience.

Chapter 4

LOWERED EXPECTATIONS
OF DISCIPLESHIP

"Jesus always comes asking disciples to follow him – not merely accept him, not merely believe in him, not merely worship him, but to follow him. One either follows Christ, or one does not. There is no compartmentalization of faith, no realm, no sphere, no business, no politic in which the lordship of Christ will be excluded. We either make him Lord of all lords, or we deny him as Lord of any."

Lee Camp

I was browsing through a bookstore when a book cover caught my eye. I realized it was one of those *How to … for Dummies* books. You've seen them, all bound with the familiar yellow and black exterior.

I must admit my wife and I have purchased a couple of these books. Like the time, Carla fell in love with a beautiful black Lab puppy. After we bought it, we realized we knew absolutely nothing about raising a Lab puppy. So, what did we do? We got a copy of *Labrador Retrievers for Dummies*.

What caught me by surprise was discovering one of these in a Christian bookstore. The title was *The Bible for Dummies*. I am not criticizing the book. Whatever will help get people engaged in Bible study is a good thing, and I am all for it. As I looked through the book, my mind drifted from its specific content to the broader challenge of discipleship. The very need for such a book exposes how little spiritual depth there is in the modern church.

The church world has been "dummying down" the definition and characteristics of discipleship for the 40 plus years I have been in ministry. I do not believe it has been intentional, but rather a reaction to the desires of the culture. I saw this dummying process escalate as "seeker friendly" churches became popular in the 1980s. Churches began to set their ministry priorities based upon the desires of a changing culture and less spiritually oriented audiences.

The focus seemed to shift from calling people to the high standard of the Scripture to "lowering the bar" in an effort not to offend anyone. This approach had some success. Many of the largest churches in America have been based on this ministry model. My concern is that in so doing, we have offered the world a substitute for discipleship.

Scripture assigns discipleship as a top priority of the church. But, based on research into the beliefs of modern

Christians, the goal of making disciples has been missed. George Barna, whose insightful analysis is used by church leaders all over the world, provides a breakdown of this evidence. In his book, *Revolution*, he reveals the following statistics:

- Only 9% of born-again believers have a biblical worldview (belief in absolute moral truth, the Bible as God's Word, Jesus's sinless life on earth, the reality of Satan, etc.).

- Fewer than one out of six church-goers have a relationship with another believer through which spiritual accountability is provided.

- The typical Christian spends less than three hours per month (outside of church services) in endeavors which develop or apply their faith.

- The church is permanently losing between 75% and 94% of its youth by their second year of college.

How could the priority of producing disciples be missed by so many churches? It is not because of a lack of programs, activities, and busyness. We have more of those than at any other time in my memory. These activities are part of the reason discipleship isn't taking place. The church has become a distracted place. I used to tell our church staff, "The main thing, is to keep the main thing, the main thing. I am concerned that churches today are so busy doing second things first, that we are facing spiritual disaster.

Charles Paul Conn, in his book *Making it Happen*, gives us a sober reminder of how distraction leads to disaster: "I read of the crash of an Eastern Airlines jumbo jet in the Florida Everglades...As the huge aircraft approached Miami Airport for its landing, a light that indicates proper deployment of the landing gear failed to come on. The plane flew in a large, looping circle over the swamps of the Everglades while the cockpit crew checked out the light failure.

"...the flight engineer fiddled with the bulb. He tried to remove it, but it wouldn't budge. Another member of the crew became curious and tried to help him out...then another. By and by, if you can believe it, all eyes were on the little bulb that refused to be dislodged. No one noticed the plane was losing altitude. Finally, it flew right into the swamp...The crew momentarily forgot the most basic of all rules in the air—don't forget to fly the airplane."

That is precisely what's happening in too many churches. We have our attention focused on the "seventy-five" cent issues that people want to argue about while the very mission Jesus gave us is crashing into our self-made swamp. The priority of our mission is displayed in the words of Jesus. He only used the phrase, "be born again" three times in His teaching. In contrast, He proclaimed, "follow me" an astonishing eighty-four times. That's right, eighty-four! For Jesus to tell us something eighty-four times, it must be important.

If the priority of Jesus was making disciples, those who are "fully devoted followers of God," why are so many in the church satisfied with so much less? The church seems so preoccupied with the "birthing process" (salvation), it often ignores the "growing process" (discipleship).

An obstetrics doctor would be sued for malpractice if he left a newborn baby to survive on his or her own, and rightly so. The public would decry such inexcusable behavior. But in the spiritual world, such abandonment is commonplace, and there is little or no outcry. Is the modern church guilty of spiritual malpractice? Such malpractice is not an offense in the legal system of our country, but God's order of accountability may not be so lenient.

The church's calling to discipleship cannot be ignored. The words of Jesus echo this mission throughout the halls of church history. One of the last statements Jesus made to his followers packs a powerful punch:

"All authority has been given to Me in heaven and on earth. Go, therefore, and make disciples of all the nations, baptizing them in the name of the Father and the Son and the Holy Spirit, teaching them to observe all that I have commanded you; and lo, I am with you always, even to the end of the age." (Matthew 28:18-20)

69

Eugene Peterson's *The Message* makes it even clearer for us: "God authorized and commanded Me to commission you: Go out and train everyone you meet, far and near, in this way of life, marking them by baptism in the three-fold name: Father, Son, and Holy Spirit. Then instruct them in the practice of all I have commanded you. I'll be with you as you do this, day after day after day, right up to the end of the age." (Matthew 28:18-20)

Many Christians have overlooked the "practicing" element of the mission Jesus gave us to fulfill. Jesus is calling those in the church to make disciples, not converts. A big reason why discipleship is neglected is that it is so time-consuming. Discipleship does not fit into the mold of our "instant results" church culture. Jesus is calling people to follow Him, not an organization, religious movement or a set of lifestyle guidelines.

The Greek word "follow" literally means "your place is following after Me (Jesus)." It conveys the idea that a disciple is committed to imitating the one being followed. In Matthew 4:19, Jesus is calling His first disciples. He calls out to Peter and Andrew as they were fishing, "Follow Me and I will make you fishers of men."

This verse has been misrepresented in most sermons I have heard. Pastors interpret it to mean making converts, but true biblical evangelism is a commitment to making disciples. "A fisher of men" is a calling to the entire process of introducing a person to Christ, teaching them His ways, and mentoring them as a devoted follower of Jesus.

C.S. Lewis said, "…. the church exists for nothing else but to draw men to Christ, to make them little Christs. If they are not doing that, all the cathedrals, clergy, missions, sermons, even the Bible itself, are simply a waste of time. God became man for no other purpose."

Anyone who knows me would confirm how much I believe in worship. But, one of the problems in the modern church is that Jesus is worshipped on Sunday, but not followed throughout the week. We all are called to be committed followers of the person, Jesus, not just intellectual or religious devotees. The Bible teaches a style of Christianity that is relationally based and follows the attitudes, actions, and works of Jesus. When a person or a church makes this commitment, it shakes up the structure of comfortable Christianity.

Church-goers who have relegated God to a "Sunday only" status spend their work week thinking, talking and acting like the culture around them. When they come to church on Sunday, they bring that cultural mindset with them. So it's no wonder that many find no value or enjoyment in the service. Like critics at a movie or concert, they assess whether the pastor was on his game today, the choir needed more practice, the worship songs were too new or too old, why the soloist wore that outfit and whether the thermostat was set correctly.

The sad reality is that many churches have not made being a disciple of Jesus a condition or characteristic of being a Christian. In his book, *The Spirit of the Disciplines*, Dallas Willard gives a clear commentary on this condition:

"One is not required to be, or even intend to be, a disciple in order to become a Christian, and one may remain a Christian without any signs of progress toward or in discipleship. Contemporary Western churches do not require following Christ in His example, spirit, and teachings as a condition of membership—either of entering or continuing in fellowship of a denomination or a local church...So far as the visible Christian institutions of our day are concerned, discipleship clearly is optional. Churches are therefore filled with 'undiscipled disciples.' Most problems in contemporary churches can be explained by the fact that members have not yet decided to follow Christ."

The issue we church leaders must discuss is how discipleship is presented as part of the salvation experience. Most sermons I have heard compartmentalize these into two separate experiences. Salvation is preached as a gift of God's grace, freely obtained by all who believe. But there is little or no mention of the commitment, sacrifice or responsibility of being a disciple. That omission sends an unspoken and unintended message that discipleship is an optional process that occurs later.

Let me be clear, salvation should never be presented in a way that it excludes discipleship. The idea that salvation is open to all, but discipleship is a separate commitment obtained by fewer people is not the gospel Jesus preached.

72

He expected every person who received His life-transforming message would become a committed follower.

I believe the perpetuation of this type of message has led the church to its current condition. Churches are filled with spiritually immature believers who have been assured they are going to heaven and that is good enough for them. But, their lifestyle and spiritual immaturity contradict the standards of being a Christian.

Dietrich Bonhoeffer was a German theologian who was executed for his faith by the Nazis in 1945 at age 39. He is quoted by John Phillips in his book, *The Form of Christ in the World: A Study of Bonhoeffer's Christology.* "Christianity without the living Christ is inevitably Christianity without discipleship ... and Christianity without discipleship is always Christianity without Christ."

The purpose of God at salvation is for every new believer to become an imitator of Christ. The priority of this lifestyle is clearly revealed to us in the Scriptures:

- *Colossians 1:10 = "Walk in a manner worthy of the Lord."*
- *Ephesians 5:1 = "Be imitators of God."*
- *Philippians 2:15 = "Prove yourselves to be blameless."*
- *1 Peter 1:15 = "Be holy in all your behavior."*
- *Ephesians 4:1 = "Walk in a manner worthy of the calling."*

The power of discipleship is the multiplying influence of one life that touches another. It is the idea that if we are asked, "What does the Kingdom of God look like"? We should be able to confidently respond, "Come and observe my life and you will see the Kingdom of God." This may sound a little arrogant, but biblically, it is not arrogant at all. As we model the life of Christ, it not only changes our life, it helps to change the lives of others. Four times in the New Testament Paul exhorts the churches, "Be imitators of me, just as I am also of Christ."

Churches are filled with those who are affiliated with true disciples but never choose to become one. In his commentary on the Gospel of Luke, scholar William Barclay describes the difference between a distant follower of Jesus and a true disciple. "It is possible to be a follower of Jesus without being a disciple; to be a camp follower without being a soldier of the King; to be a hanger-on in some great work without pulling one's weight. Once someone was talking to a great scholar about a younger man; He said, "So and so tells me he was one of your students." The teacher answered devastatingly, 'He may have attended my lectures, but he was not one of my students.' There is a world of difference between attending lectures and being a student. It is one of the supreme handicaps of the church that in the church there are so many distant followers of Jesus and so few real disciples."

A few years ago, I attended a meeting where a discussion of this problem was taking place. The late Bob

Warren, a dear friend who led a discipleship ministry in Kentucky, made a statement that shocked me. He said, "Among attendees in most churches only three out of one hundred will actually grasp the message and have the spiritual desire to become committed disciples." When he said it, I responded, "Oh come on Bob, that can't be right." Part of my response was because I didn't want it to be right. If it were right, I would have to take some responsibility since I was the leader of the church. We have discussed that statistic many times since that day. Even though I did not want it to be true, I began to observe those in the church more closely. It saddens me to admit it, but Bob was not far off in his assessment. So I ask, why?

One glaring factor is that we have accepted a gospel without evidence of transformation. The word "transformation" comes from the Greek word that is the origin of our English word, "metamorphosis." It is a combination of two words, "meta" which means "to change or transform" and "morphe" which means "form." This gives us our English definition; "to change in outward appearance, form, and character."

The metamorphosis of the butterfly is an excellent analogy for what occurs in a Christian's life at salvation. This is beautifully described by Neil Anderson and Robert Saucy in their book, *The Common Made Holy*.

"Consider the plight of the caterpillar. It crawls on the surface of the earth with tiny suction cup-like legs ... One day, as though led by instinct, it climbs as high as it can by its own strength—usually on the limb of a tree or on a small branch. There it sews a little button that forms an attachment for the cocoon that it spins around itself as it hangs upside down. The caterpillar ceases to exist, and a miraculous transformation takes place. In the caterpillar's place, there is now a butterfly that eventually fights its way out and learns to fly. The caterpillar 'crucified' itself to be 'resurrected' a butterfly. It gave up the security of its own limited resources and earthbound existence to fly in the heavenlies. Though a caterpillar would appear to be much stronger than a butterfly, it cannot escape the law of gravity. The butterfly is the more fragile creature, but it can gracefully soar in freedom. The caterpillar gave up all that it was to become all that the Creator designed for it to become."

All believers experience a metamorphosis at the moment of salvation, but the transforming work of the Spirit continues to operate. In Paul's letter to the Corinthian church, he said, "But, we all with unveiled face, beholding as in a mirror the glory of the Lord, are being transformed into the same image from glory to glory, just as from the Lord, the Spirit" (2 Corinthians 3:18).

The power of transformation must be presented as part of the salvation experience. If it is not, we are presenting an incomplete picture of the gospel. The way we live on the outside is an indication of what exists on the inside. "Therefore, if anyone is in Christ, he is a new creature; the old things passed away; behold, new things have come" (2

Corinthians 5:17). Where is the evidence of the "new things" in the lives of the people sitting in the pews on Sunday? It should concern us greatly when their lifestyle is no different from that of non-Christians.

The church is so quick to place the "backslidden" label on people. Now, don't get me wrong. It is possible for Christians to make bad decisions, fail morally, struggle with addictions, experience divorce and a myriad of failings. But, how do we explain the person who has never exhibited any characteristics of the new life that occurs at salvation? How can we label this person as backslidden? One must have made significant forward progress before they can slide back. When the church labels people who have never experienced any change as backslidden, it does one of two things. First, it props up a false security about their salvation. Second, it promotes a "victim" view of salvation.

Neil Anderson writes in *The Common Made Holy*, "Now, imagine what would happen to the growth of the new butterfly if it chose to believe it was still a caterpillar and walked instead of flying. He would come nowhere near to reaching his potential. Likewise, when we who are new in Christ perceive we are still the old self, we won't experience the fullness of the Christian life … If we think and act like caterpillars, the Lord will receive no glory for what He did on our behalf."

Throughout Jesus' ministry and continuing throughout the rest of the New Testament, the word "disciple" is used 267 times. The word "Christian" is only used three times. It is obvious the recurring theme of God's heart is becoming and making disciples.

The word disciple comes from the Greek word *mathetes*, which is translated literally as a "learner." All disciples start at the same place as learners of Jesus. As I study the life of Jesus, I see three main values in His way of making disciples:

1. He operated in the context of relationships

Relationships, which are authentic life connections based on Christ-like love, are the environment for effective discipleship. The spiritual journey becomes about more than attending a meeting; it is about living life together with others. Without loving relationships, there is no true discipleship, only the passing of information.

It is one thing to attend a church meeting and listen to the experiences of others. It is quite another to be taught about Jesus by people who know you, love you and are committed to your spiritual well-being. In this atmosphere, one can ask questions, confess sin, practice accountability, give and receive encouragement and build trust.

The relationships Jesus developed with His disciples were grounded in unconditional love. "A new command I give you: Love one another As I have loved you, so you must love one another By this all men will know that you are my disciples, if you love one another" (John 13:34-35 NIV). Jesus' example proves that Christ-like love is not just the environment for effective discipleship, it is also the evidence of discipleship.

2. He provided an opportunity to put truth into practice

Jesus did not protect His disciples from real life in the safety of a classroom cocoon. Most of their training was "on-the-job" as they walked through life together. My pastoral experience has led me to conclude we have inverted the leadership model of Jesus. We inundate our people with information about church services, Bible studies, small groups, Sunday school, retreats, camps, conferences, etc. By contrast, the discipleship style of Jesus was 90% active training and 10% instruction. Most churches use a process of 90% instruction and 10% "on-your-own" training and experience.

As I look back, I clearly understand why I, like so many pastors, was drawn to the information style of discipleship. It is much easier to deliver a lesson or sermon than to daily invest in the lives of disciples. This has led us to an unhealthy view of spiritual growth (that the congregation is maturing as they hear more sermons). Jesus knew the disciples. He was preparing them to lead the church He was leaving behind. Day by day, He taught and mentored them; He confronted and rebuked them; He encouraged and motivated them; He inspired them and then He released them. The world became their laboratory to practice what they had been taught by Jesus and to do the things they observed Him doing. Whenever the disciples failed in what they had been sent to do, Jesus turned it into a teaching moment. Sometimes He rebuked them, but He never condemned them. He provided a safe place for His disciples to attempt great things. He allowed them to fail safely, to learn what went wrong and try it again.

Jesus could have done all the work Himself, but that would not have multiplied the effectiveness of the Kingdom. Instead, He empowered imperfect people by giving them God-sized assignments.

3. He modeled authenticity through accountability

Like all good leaders, Jesus gave his disciples assignments and responsibilities. He always guided them with clear instructions (such as where to find a donkey for his ride into Jerusalem, how to prepare the Passover, and how the Seventy were to be sent out). And as the Parable of the Talents shows, He expected good results from those entrusted with Kingdom assignments. Jesus never left His disciples on their own to figure things out for themselves. When the disciples returned from an assignment, He made sure they understood each task's Kingdom implications.

Jesus helped the disciples realize they were primarily responsible to God, the audience of one, the Creator of life. Love motivated them to give an account of their lives and to work for eternity. By contrast, religious and governmental authorities of the day forced accountability by threats of punishment and shame. Jesus shows us that such motivation is not authentic accountability at all.

Being the salt of the earth as Jesus describes, cannot be

experienced in a salt-shaker. Many years ago, I found myself unnaturally attached to the salt-shaker. I was so sermon and teaching-focused that I convinced myself these efforts were enough to make disciples. The misconception was made worse by well-meaning people in the church applauding my efforts. As the years passed, I found myself less fulfilled, while losing passion and feeling detached.

Thankfully, J.R. Woodward at Dream Awakener helped get my perspective on track. His post *"A Working Definition of Success,"* helped me understand how to function with a disciple-oriented value system. He asks pastors,

- *Not how many people come to our church services, but how many people our church serves?*

- *Not how many people attend our ministry, but how many people have we equipped for ministry?*

- *Not how many people minister inside the church, but how many minister outside the church?*

- *Not how many ministries we start, but how many ministries we help?*

- *Not how many unbelievers we bring into the community of faith, but how many "believers" we help experience healthy community?*

- *Not what resources God gives us to steward, but how many good stewards are we developing for the sake of the world?*

- *Not how we are connecting with our culture but how we are engaging our culture?*

- *Not how effective we are with our mission, but how faithful we are to our God?*

- *Not how unified our local church is, but how unified is "the church" in our neighborhood, city, and world?*

- *Not how much we immerse ourselves in the text, but how faithfully do we live in the story of God.*

In a disciple-oriented Christian context, the central issue is maturation. Are we growing in every aspect of our life? Are we becoming more like Jesus? Are we blessing the world as the people of God? The maturation process is often messy; it takes time. But there is no necessary correlation between time logged sitting in pews and attaining godliness. Maturation occurs in an atmosphere where accountability is expected and practiced. In this environment, people are challenged, coached and celebrated in their spiritual journeys.

When I look back over my years of ministry, I conclude that some form of "small group" format provides the most beneficial environment for the process of developing disciples. Every church regardless of denomination, structure or size can develop and implement a format of small groups to facilitate discipleship. The key is to maintain the priority of developing mature disciples. I find Christians who come from this type of emphasis, are healthier. A "disciple focused" small group ministry can help us model the priority of relationships, grow larger by growing smaller and provide a safe and loving environment of accountability. Small groups nurture spiritual growth, encouraging each person to individual commitment and mutual corporate involvement that help the church become all God intended.

Personal Inventory

Answer each question based on what is true today in your life. This will point out places you need to adjust your perspective and experience. If unsure, answer what is predominantly true.

1. I believe Jesus is more interested in followers than converts.

2. I agree that making disciples is the mission of those in the church.

3. I am currently involved in a discipling relationship.

4. I agree that Jesus has the expectation of every believer becoming a disciple.

5. I realize that I am to be personally involved in helping others become disciples.

6. I understand that "making disciples" does not occur by just attending a church service.

7. I agree that evangelism alone is not enough.

8. I believe a disciple should imitate or model the character of Christ.

9. I am personally imitating the reality of Christ in my life and relationships.

10. I will assist my church in its efforts to develop disciples.

Count the number of "yes" answers and number of "no" answers. If you have more "no" answers than "yes" answers, you need to re-evaluate your view of discipleship as it relates to your church experience.

Chapter 5

INFLUENCE OF CONSUMERISM

"The widest thing in the universe is not space; it is the potential capacity of the human heart. Being made in the image of God, it is capable of almost unlimited extension in all directions. And one of the world's greatest tragedies is that we allow our hearts to shrink until there is room in them for little besides ourselves."

A.W.Tozer

In the early 1970s, Burger King was trying to find their niche in the competitive fast food market. To break free from the prevailing image of assembly line fast food, they introduced the slogan, "Have it your way," and let customers customize their burgers. The "Have it your way" message soon became identified with Burger King Restaurants worldwide.

This slogan now reflects the prevailing consumerist mindset in our culture. What do we mean by consumerism? My definition is: *"the mindset that is preoccupied with self-interest, seeks to be served, looks for facets of society that can provide services for personal benefit and elevates personal needs and pursuits above what others may require."*

That philosophy is clearly evident in our culture. Every TV commercial or program, every store, every movie, every car or clothing product, every website, every restaurant now aims to fit the customer's desire, need or personal preference. The frustrating pitfall of this mentality is that it's never enough. Eventually, the house or the car or our clothes get older, and we want new ones. This is how we are wired to think in our culture. It is all justified by the rationale of "You're worth it. You deserve to have what you want, how you want it when you want it."

Modern Christianity plays the same game and communicates the same philosophy. We try to provide as comfortable an experience as humanly possible, using every means at our disposal to attract crowds of people. That's Marketing 101, right? The problem is, at the end of the day, the only thing that Jesus is counting is disciples. By nature, disciples are producers, not consumers. Yet most of our churches are built around feeding consumers. Based on my personal experience I estimate 80 to 90 percent of a church's time, energy and resources are linked to attracting and satisfying spiritual consumers.

If you use consumerist methods to attract people to your church, you must continue using them to keep them interested or else they will find another church to meet their "needs." This consumer mentality is a contradiction to the gospel and to the call of discipleship. Disciples aren't consumers who need to be catered to, they are followers who serve and produce. It's one thing to be creative, innovative and relevant in presenting the gospel to our culture, but we can't serve all the whims of the consumer mentality.

You may be asking, "Ok, what does this have to do with me?" More than you think. Let's examine how the consumer mindset is undermining the teachings of Jesus and the mission of the church.

1. Self-oriented personal choices

Spiritual leaders in 21st Century America are attempting to lead people who are presented with choices for every decision of their lives. These choices are being influenced by pitchmen (and women) persuading them that various product choices will improve their quality of life. Rarely do the biblical concepts of responsibility, service or sacrifice enter the message because they run counter to the desire for personal freedom and fulfillment.

The appeal to individual desire and fulfillment is the language of our times. But biblically, we in the church have one choice: to follow God wholeheartedly. He gave us His perspective on personal choice in the book of Deuteronomy:

"...I have set before you life and death, the blessing and the curse. So **choose** life in order that you may live, you and your descendants, **loving** the Lord your God, and by **obeying** His voice, and **holding** fast to Him."

(Deuteronomy 30: 19-20b—emphasis mine)

2. A diminished view of scriptural authority

Me-first consumerism causes people to question and reject scriptural authority. A church leader should be judged on whether he or she is acting within the bounds of Scripture. But today, the Bible is ignored when it conflicts with something that benefits the consumer/churchgoer.

In our present spiritual climate, faith is exchanged for instant gratification, biblical life principles yield to urges of the moment, and servanthood is considered foolish. This reminds me of the warning Paul gave to young Timothy, "The time will come when they will not endure sound doctrine; but wanting to have their ears tickled, will accumulate for themselves teachers in accordance with their own desires, and will turn away from the truth and will turn aside to myths" (2Timothy 4:3-4).

Not only has there been a shift in the way spiritual truth is received and applied but how it is presented. Teachings on sin, redemption, righteousness, transformation and the reality of hell have given way to those on personal fulfillment and self-advancement. The pseudo-physiological has taken over the theological. The real authority has become the consumer. His/her choices or personal perception of happiness ("what works for me") determine the validity of the message.

3. Acceptance of moral relativism

This worldview holds that there is no singular truth. Therefore, everyone is free to choose their own version of what is true or moral. Those who hold this view see their "truth" as equally valid as the Bible or other religious precepts. While this view is not obvious in most churches, it has infected them because of the "Have it your way" effects of consumerism.

Many pastors have been caught off guard by the average church attendee's drift into moral relativism. We have churches full of people who claim to value Scripture, but easily pick and choose the aspects of it they will apply to their lives. Usually, the choice they make is based on what they perceive will suit them then.

Again, personal happiness is the goal, not based on the Bible, but based on personal desires, feelings, and emotions. In the Old Testament, Solomon gives clear counsel:

"There is a way which seems right to a man, but its end is the way of death" (Proverbs 14:12).

"The way of a fool is right in his own eyes, but a wise man is he who listens to counsel" (Proverbs 12:15).

"Every man's way is right in his own eyes, but the Lord weighs the hearts (motives)" (Proverbs 21:2).

4. Rejection of spiritual discipline

Consumerism teaches people the right to choose is the ultimate expression of personhood and individuality. Any form of correction, regardless of its biblical basis, is considered an attempt to take away their freedom. They believe no one should tell them how to live. Accountability and discipline have become near impossible except in cases of obvious, glaring sin. Even then, it is difficult. Our acceptance of behavior among Christians that contradicts Scripture has compromised the authenticity of the church because the boundaries have been removed. Jesus gave precise instructions for dealing with practices within the church that require discipline.

"And if your brother sins go and reprove him in private; if he listens to you, you have won your brother. But if he does not listen to you, take one or two more with you, so that by the mouth of two or three witnesses every fact may be confirmed. And if he refuses to listen to them, tell it to the church; and if he refuses to listen to the church, let him be to you as a gentile (heathen) and a tax-gather" (Matthew 18:15-17).

One of the hardest things in pastoral ministry is to bring correction to Christians who have fallen in their spiritual life. The scope the failures I've encountered has encompassed every situation imaginable. Some of these required church leadership to discipline the offender. It always surprises me when the discipline imposed causes a greater uproar than the failure itself. Rather than seeing the restriction as a way of helping the person overcome sin and restore relationship, their friends and family become angry at leadership for being "too tough, uncaring or judgmental." I have seen people leave the church rather than face the problem. Sadly, the issue often resurfaces when they move to another place to avoid accountability.

5. Pursuit of happiness

The U.S. Declaration of Independence states, "We hold these truths to be self-evident, that all men are created equal, that they are endowed by their Creator with certain unalienable Rights, that among these are Life, Liberty and the pursuit of Happiness…" Americans may not live up to the standard of the document as a whole, but the "pursuit of happiness" has been thoroughly embraced. It has infiltrated every institution in our culture.

When parents are asked, "What do you want for your children?" Typical responses are something like, "I don't care what they choose to do; I just want them to be happy." This mentality is going to be the epitaph of the consumer generation.

This philosophy is choking the life out of Christian marriages and ruining their witness of love and faithfulness. I cannot estimate the number of marriages that have ended because one spouse thought a new partner was the key to achieving happiness. To make the situation worse, many in the church have convinced themselves that this thinking is within the will of God.

I have sat in so many marital counseling sessions trying to prevent another casualty. When things get difficult, and changes must be made, one spouse will inevitably say, "Well, I'm just not happy in this marriage, and I don't believe God wants marriage to be like this. I believe God wants me to be happy." The actual wording changes from case to case, but the distorted view of God's character remains the same. Does it never occur to them that God may be more concerned with their character than their happiness!

This thinking also affects our values. If we avoid situations that challenge our character or do not bring instant personal satisfaction, what chance do we have to become disciples of Christ? Jesus contradicted consumerist ideology when He told His disciples: "If anyone wishes to come after Me, he must deny himself, and take up his cross, and follow Me" (Luke 9:23).

I doubt He meant for us to follow Him in a van loaded with happiness-producing material things (our big screen TV, boat, easy chair, favorite foods, etc. I also doubt He meant we are to follow Him from church to church in search of the congregation that best "meets our needs."

Yet, it seems that few church leaders will challenge this perspective because they know if they do, it will spark opposition. In the modern church, we do not like our idols to be tipped over. So, we church leaders give in to the appetite of the consumer. To grow the church, we put in a new coffee bar, more comfortable seats, new video screens, more parking, laser lighting, smoke machines, etc. We justify self-serving choices with the skewed view that God's grace covers our pursuit of happiness.

6. Spectator congregation

The heart of New Testament Christianity is servanthood. This is what Jesus taught and modeled to His disciples. He said, "Whoever wishes to be great among you shall be your servant" (Matthew 20:26). Paul confirmed this saying, "...through love, serve one another" (Galatians. 5:13).

Consumerism has so blinded Christians that we no longer see the church and others through the eyes of a servant. People now look for churches or decide to stay at a church based on a cafeteria-style appetite. We walk through the serving line of spiritual dishes, and we pick and choose what we like and what we want. If it doesn't meet our expectation, we complain until someone satisfies our desires.

One of the great frustrations I experience as a pastor is the confusing excuses people give for changing churches. The one that absolutely drives me nuts is, "Pastor, it is nothing personal, we love you, but we do not feel we are being fed." What? Nothing personal; how much more personal can it be? There is nothing more personal than the calling and work of God in a pastor's life. The things that flow out of his heart in ministry reflect what God is doing in him personally. So, how can it not be personal when it is used as a reason to leave the church? The "I'm not being fed" statement has become the catch-all excuse for leaving a church. Typically the departing person has no reason, or won't be honest about why.

Over the years, I have gained some insight into this statement. When people only eat one meal a week, they will be malnourished. When the pastor's sermon or a Sunday school class are the only spiritual food being consumed during a week, people look at the "feeding machine" as the problem, rather than the need to feed themselves more often.

Consumerism has changed the church from being a Body of servants to a collection of spectators. What does a spectator do? They watch! They are not in the arena, attempting to make a difference. Spectators sit in the stands and tell the ones doing the work, how they could have done the work better.

Theodore Roosevelt, the 26th president of the United States, once gave a speech in Paris that still rings with truth a century later: "It is not the critic who counts; not the man who points out how the strong man stumbles, or where the doer of deeds could have done them better. The credit belongs to the man who is actually in the arena, whose face is marred by dust and sweat and blood, who strives valiantly; who errs and comes short again and again; because there is not effort without error and shortcomings; but who does actually strive to do the deed; who knows the great enthusiasm, the great devotion, who spends himself in a worthy cause, who at the best knows in the end the triumph of high achievement and who at the worst, if he fails, at least he fails while daring greatly. So, that his place shall never be with those cold and timid souls who know neither victory nor defeat."

It amazes me how differently people treat pastors than those in other professional occupations. They would never think of telling their doctor, mechanic, plumber, accountant, contractor, banker, etc. how to do their job. But, when it comes to church ministry and leadership, the voice of the spectators can be heard loud and clear. The church seems to be the only place in our culture where years of experience and training are expected to be subservient to those who have neither.

A spectator comes to be entertained and expects the show to be good. And if it isn't, they leave and find a better show. Membership additions in the typical American church today are more often from people moving from one church to another, rather than the result of outreach, evangelism or discipleship. So the modern church is continually trading sheep.

7. Loss of lordship

When we approach Christianity from a consumer perspective rather than as lifestyle based on biblical values and beliefs, we demote Jesus from His rightful position as Lord of our life. The church becomes just another "add-on" in our life, a product or service we consume like

Starbucks or Apple. We no longer represent our Christian faith by obedience, good works, and righteousness, but instead by consumption of Christian merchandise and activities.

That would explain why many Americans who identify themselves as "born-again" Christians live no differently than their unchurched neighbors. Obedience should be the evidence of our faith. Jesus said, "If anyone loves Me, he will keep My word; and My Father will love him, and we will come to him, and make Our abode with him. He who does not love Me does not keep My words; and the word which you hear is not Mine, but the Father's who sent Me" (John 14:23-24). He also said, "You are My friends if you do what I command you" (John 15:14).

When we no longer view Jesus as "Lord," it distorts our view of everything else. Pollster George Barna writes, "Most churchgoers have not adopted a biblical worldview; they have simply added a Jesus fish bumper sticker on the bumper of one of their other consumer identities."

8. Forfeiture of spiritual freedom

Consumerism undermines the freedom we have in our relationship with Christ. It denies His all sufficiency in our life. It tries to trick us into believing that life as a Christian is incomplete, and our fulfillment depends on adding the cultural trinkets the world values. Paul wrote a stern warning to the Colossian Christians about the dangers of this philosophy: "See to it that no one takes you captive

97

through philosophy and empty deception, according to the tradition of men, according to the elementary principles of the world, rather than according to Christ" (Colossians 2:8).

The deceptive nature of materialism is what causes well-meaning Christians to forfeit their spiritual freedom. Most churchgoers are so blinded by their pursuit of personal fulfillment that they are unaware they have become ensnared. If they truly understood, they would cry out to God and return to the path of grace.

Paul rebuked the Galatians when they were being lured away from Christ, and he challenged them to not give away their spiritual freedom. "But now that you have come to know God, or rather to be known by God, how is it that you turn back again to the weak and worthless elemental things, to which you desire to be enslaved all over again?" (Galatians 4:9).

9. Spiritual manipulation

A Christian who keeps pursuing personal desires demonstrates he does not know or understand the character of God. Our Lord is a loving and generous Father, but He demands faith and obedience from all who receive Him. Some preachers have developed theologies which make it seem we can get God to bless us if we follow the right steps. The Lord does bless us and prosper us, but we are wrong to ever think we can control and manipulate Him! Entire church movements have been built around this mindset.

The consumerist philosophy is on full display in churches that preach that God's primary desire is for His followers to have an abundance of material possessions. In these churches, pastors lead the way by acquiring yachts, luxury vehicles, mansions, planes, etc. Jesus could have possessed great earthly wealth, but instead, He modeled a life of simplicity and servanthood.

I understand that all ministries have financial requirements and that budgets must be met by donors who believe in what they do. But, caution needs to be taken in the way we present the character of God amid a culture dominated by consumerism. It's a grave error to believe we can earn God's favor and blessing by donating lots of money. God does bless generosity, but we cannot treat God as though He were running a department store. When that occurs, pastors become like clerks who take people's money and dispense the goods they desire.

10. Substitutional Identity

Consumerism attacks the most important part of a Christian's transformed life: our spiritual identity. It is the foundation upon which our spiritual life is built. Spiritual identity refers to a person's "position in Christ" after experiencing salvation.

When a person receives Christ, the "old man" (dominated by sin) is transformed into a "new man" (receiving righteousness from God). That means Christians' perspectives of themselves, their values, and their worldview have changed from dependence on self to rely on the full sufficiency of Christ. The New Testament amply describes this spiritual transaction:

> We are rescued from sin through forgiveness—Colossians 1:13-14
>
> We become righteous before God—2 Corinthians 5:21
>
> We experience a divine change of nature—1 Peter 1:2-4
>
> We are made spiritually alive—Ephesians 2:1-6
>
> We are reconciled with God in a personal relationship—Colossians 1:21-22
>
> We continue to be transformed into Christ's image—2 Corinthians 3:18
>
> We are empowered by God's Spirit—John 15:5

When Christians fail to live their true spiritual identity, they live in denial of their new nature. As author Gary Thomas describes it, "Instead of being motivated by a glorious, eternal plan based on being loved and loving in return, we spend our days in trivial, selfish, self-absorbed pursuits." The subtle danger of consumerism is that it denies God's standards and provides substitutes in line with the culture. Consumerism reinforces a value system that is opposed to spiritual reality.

Consumerism also has given birth to an attitude of entitlement which has become a plague to our culture. The tragic outcome of this mentality is that nothing is ever enough. It places people in a perpetual condition of discontent. Materialistic thinking makes us unable to recognize the blessings of God and rest in them because we are driven to have more and more of our desires fulfilled. This culture ridicules the biblical concept of contentment as being willing to "settle for less" than they deserve.

With this view of life, things become more important than people and having is more important than being. It becomes a lifestyle that pursues distraction rather than truth and substitutes desire for personal responsibility.

This is the source of the "commitment vacuum" facing the average church. Consumers do not share in responsibilities and obligations to their fellow consumers. And churches today are increasingly occupied by consumerists who take more than they give. This mindset also has led to a decreased commitment to priorities such as family, friendships, and community service.

The Prophet Haggai issued a stern warning that still speaks to our consumerist culture: "Now this is what the Lord Almighty says; Give careful thought to your ways. You have planted much, but have harvested little. You eat but never have enough. You drink but never have your fill. You put on clothes but are not warm. You earn wages, only to put them in a purse with holes in it" (Haggai 1:5-6 NIV).

There are growing numbers of Christians who are tired of the frustration, discouragement, despair, and emptiness that consumerism brings. For many, especially younger Christians, the influence of consumerism is all they have ever known. When they hear that it conflicts with a biblical worldview, they are confused. However, amid the confusion their heart cries out, "There must be more to life than this."

I believe this understanding is the first step toward breaking the stronghold of consumerism. This generation needs to hear about the joy and satisfaction of giving instead of taking, of serving instead of being served, of showing love and kindness without expecting anything in return. We pastors need to lead the way by showing, not just telling our people how to invest our lives in a cause bigger than ourselves.

This became abundantly clear to me after I became pastor of a small congregation in East Texas. Within three years the church grew to several hundred people, but as we grew, our focus became more inward than outward. Our church leadership recognized we had to get the congregation to invest in a cause bigger than ourselves.

One of our strategies was to launch a ministry that served the needs of our community in practical ways. We named it Nehemiah Network which was based on the work of Nehemiah rebuilding the wall of Jerusalem. Our only agenda was to show the love of God practically. We mobilized teams throughout the community assisting single mothers, senior citizens and the disabled with yard work, minor house repairs and general cleaning. All services were provided without charge and without advertising the name of the church.

The impact on the lives of the people in our church was incredible. For many, it was the first time they had given of themselves so freely. It created a momentum of creativity throughout the church. The focus shifted from what we could accomplish for our own benefit to creating new ways of serving people outside the church. One team approached the church leadership with the vision of developing a Family Food Center. The church embraced the idea and took our biggest classroom and turned it into a food distribution center. The congregation began actively bringing and donating food items. At the same time, a sizable chunk of the church budget was allocated to purchase food each week to be given away. The center helped approximately 70 families every week, and the spiritual influence was overwhelming.

This affirmed to me how important it is for people in the church to get a vision of life beyond the pursuit of their own desires. They learned that God has a purpose for each person bigger than anything the culture can provide.

When I think about the subtlety of consumerism, I

recall the challenging words of Jim Elliott, a missionary killed by the Auca Indians. He declared, "He is no fool who gives what he cannot keep to gain what he cannot lose."

That should be our answer to consumerism!

Personal Inventory

Answer each question based on what is true today in your life. This will point out places you need to adjust your perspective and experience. If unsure, answer what is predominantly true.

1. I realize that living as a consumer is a form of selfishness.

2. I view the church as an opportunity to "give and serve" rather than "take and get."

3. I accept that my happiness is not God's ultimate goal.

4. I understand the church does not exist for me and to solely meet individual needs.

5. I voluntarily submit to the decisions of church leadership.

6. I know my spiritual gift and function in the church within that capacity.

7. I am sensitive to the needs of others and look for ways to serve them.

8. I am tolerant of others and treat their interests with equal value as my own.

9. I agree that consumerism is a mindset of the flesh and not of the Spirit.

10. I believe consumerism is focused on the temporal instead of the eternal.

Count the number of "yes" answers and number of "no" answers. If you have more "no" answers than "yes" answers, you need to re-evaluate your view of consumerism as it relates to your church experience.

Chapter 6

MISPLACED PRIORITY OF WORSHIP

"On Sundays God wants us to do more than sing songs together and have wonderful worship experiences. He wants to knit the fabric of our lives together. For many, church has become all about me – what I'm learning, what I'm seeking, what I'm desperate for, what I need, how I've been affected, what I can do. We see ourselves as isolated individuals all seeking personal encounters with God, wherever we can find them. This reflects our individualistic, me-obsessed culture. Rather than seeing ourselves as part of a worship community, we become worship consumers. We want worship on demand, served up in our own time, and with our own music."

Bob Kauflin

Author of *True Worshipers*

While Jesus was traveling with His disciples, they entered a village that was home to sisters Mary and Martha. After welcoming Jesus into their home, a vivid scene unfolds between the two sisters and Jesus. In Luke 10, Mary is described as sitting at the feet of Jesus listening,

107

while Martha is working hard doing the preparations of a gracious hostess. In most sermons I have heard, Mary is portrayed as the heroine of the story. They question how Martha could get so distracted from the presence of Jesus. But think about it. Martha had just welcomed Jesus, the Messiah, into their home. What host wouldn't want every detail just right? We do the same thing with people we wish to honor.

During the presidential election of 1992, I had the opportunity to be Master of Ceremonies in a campaign event for President George H.W. Bush. I felt new empathy for Martha as I learned first-hand about the amount of preparation required for a visitor of such importance. The Secret Service scrutinized every aspect of the event; as did the President's staff. It was quite memorable but also incredibly stressful. So it is easy for me to understand Martha's preoccupation with all the details she saw as necessary. But her distraction caused her to make a critical error in her perspective.

Luke 10:41-42 says, "But Martha was distracted with all her preparations; and she came up to Him and said, Lord, do you not care that my sister has left me to do all the serving alone? Then tell her to help me. But the Lord answered and said to her, Martha, Martha, you are worried and bothered about so many things; but only one thing is necessary, for Mary has chosen the good part, which shall not be taken away from her."

In our culture, we believe we are accomplishing the

most important things in life by staying busy, but often the opposite is true. I believe this is one of the key reasons for such frustration and weariness in the church. In the little booklet, *The Tyranny of the Urgent*, Charles Hummel describes the problem this way:

"When we stop long enough to think about it, we realize that our dilemma goes deeper than a shortage of time; it is basically a problem of priorities ... We sense uneasily our failure to do what was really important. The winds of other people's demands and not our own inner compulsions have driven us onto a reef of frustration."

Jesus was not telling Martha that her preparations were unimportant. But, they were not to be her priority. The top priority was what Mary had already discovered—spending time in the presence of Jesus. When Christians begin substituting the urgent for the important, we give priority to our programs, activities, and achievements. The result is emptiness and spiritual weariness. When the church tries to be all things to all people, it distracts us from what distinguishes it from all other institutions—**Worship!**

Author Gordon Dahl gives an insightful analysis in his book, *Work, Play and Worship in a Leisure-Oriented Society*: "Most middle-class Americans tend to worship their work, to work at their play and play at their worship. As a result, their meanings and values are distorted. Their relationships disintegrate faster than they can keep them in repair and their lifestyles resemble a cast of characters in search of a plot."

God never intended for us to live on such a horizontal level. When we only respond to what's achievable, what's logical and what's practical, we neglect the essential vertical relationship in our life. God designed us to be fulfilled through His Word, His Presence, and His Priorities. The goal of all that God has given us is **Worship!**

It is embarrassing to admit that the first 15 years of my pastoral career were horizontally focused. I was trained in a denomination that embraced performance-based ministry. I was judged on what I could produce for the church. There was little emphasis on life transformation, intimacy with God or the Presence of God. I worked hard to get results but received harsh judgment when I fell short of expectations.

I felt myself becoming two different people. The outward man was jumping through the hoops and being cheered for apparent success, but the inner man was dying. After a series of circumstances, I was terminated from my church staff position after nine years. I knew I was at a crossroad moment in my individual life and ministry. There just had to be a better way and if I couldn't find it, I didn't want to be in ministry any longer.

Then in the summer of 1987, God did something I didn't expect. I was attending a three-day music festival called "Jesus Go Fest" at the Youth With A Mission campus near Lindale, Texas. It was three days of worship, speakers, workshops and mission opportunities. I had never been in that kind of ministry environment before, but God had me right where He wanted me. One of the musicians was Sheila Walsh, and during her song set, she made a statement that God used to transform my spiritual journey and ministry. It may have been a transitional thought for her, but it was transformational for me. She said, "God has many servants, but He doesn't have many friends."

Wow! I had never considered the possibility of being God's friend. That night began a journey for me of focusing on being God's friend and allowing my other service to freely flow out of a relationship with Him. I have learned through the years that God is not nearly as interested in my performing for Him as He is in my worship of Him.

The priority of being a worshipper is clearly stated by Jesus in His encounter with the Samaritan woman. "But an hour is coming, and now is, when true worshippers will worship the Father in Spirit and in truth; for such people the Father seeks to be His worshippers. God is spirit, and those who worship Him must worship in spirit and truth" (John 4:23-24).

Imagine that! God is pursuing us. He is not seeking our abilities, He is seeking our worship! God loves it when we worship Him, and when we are focused on Him, everything else in life pales in comparison. One of the best definitions of worship I've seen comes from Charles Swindoll's book, *The Church Awakening.*

"The Hebrew term for *worship* has at its root the action of bowing down. Interestingly, the root Greek word for worship, *proskuneo,* refers to the custom of "prostrating one's self before a person and kissing his feet," which carries the idea of giving honor. Our English word worship comes from the old Anglo-Saxon term *weorthscipe or* "worth-ship" which means, "to attribute worth to someone or something.

"Therefore, when referring to the worship of God, it is attributing supreme worth to Him who alone is worthy of our praise and honor. Worship underscores our celebration of everything that brings honor to our God. In giving Him honor—when we have truly worshipped—there is something so deeply satisfying and gratifying about the experience that mere words cannot adequately describe it."

So, it stands to reason that the church should be a place of worship and a gathering of worshippers. All Christians need to understand that God loves worship! Eternity is filled with worship! The characteristic that should distinguish Christians from everyone else in the world is worship! I love the vivid imagery of the exchange between Moses and God in Exodus 33. After a time of prayer, God answers Moses in verse 14 by saying, "...My presence shall go with you, and I will give you rest." Moses then responds with a statement that should be the guiding principle for our lives today. In verse 15-16, he says, "...If your presence does not go with us, do not lead us up from here. For how then can it be known that I have found favor in Your sight,

I and Your people? Is it not by Your going with us, so that we, I and Your people, may be distinguished from all the other people who are upon the face of the earth?"

Did you get what Moses was saying? God's presence is what distinguishes His people from the rest of the world. That is why the anthem of the church of Jesus Christ must be worship!

Even though the Bible affirms worship as the church's priority, it has become one of the most contentious issues in the church today. As a pastor, I have found myself on the front lines of this battle, and I have the scars to prove it. I sometimes feel like I have spent my entire ministry in the worship transition battle. In the first church I pastored, we went through a complete transition from worship centered on a piano and organ with a choir to a contemporary style with a full band and no choir. You can imagine the challenge of that time!

In the second church I pastored, the worship transition had started before I arrived. We finalized the shift from a Southern Gospel style of worship to a blended style which included both contemporary songs and a few old hymns.

I am often asked which transition was the most difficult since the outcome was somewhat different. Both were painful, but the pain was different. In the transition to full contemporary, when the process was completed, the identity of the church was set. We did not have to fight the battle anymore. In the transition to a more blended style, we never seemed to get to the finish line. We just frustrated people on both sides of the issue. The problem with trying to achieve a "middle of the road" position, is you get rocks thrown at you from both sides.

Change is never easy, and I have found this to be especially true when it comes to worship. Much has been written about this issue, so obviously, I am not going to reconcile the differences among believers in the brief pages of this chapter. However, I believe it is essential to discuss the effect this battle is having on the church and to ask ourselves some hard questions.

If God is seeking worshippers, and we in the church are distinguished by worship, shouldn't there be some common ground from which we can discuss this issue? What is the battle over worship producing in our churches? How is it affecting our spiritual health? What are we promoting as Christian priorities? What values are we celebrating?

I believe we have ample common ground to achieve unity. But in churches nationwide, sides are still being taken, biblical arguments are being made, and casualties are mounting. Regardless of your personal worship preference, we cannot continue to engage in this battle. The damage is too great. Let's examine the destructive impact of this conflict:

1. _Christians have developed a distorted view of worship_

The very term "worship" has come to be identified with an event we attend. Churches call their weekly gathering the "worship service." We prepare church bulletins that contain the "order of worship." There are traditional rituals referred to as the "call to worship." We design campaigns to attract people to our "worship experience." There is nothing wrong with any of these things. But, in a culture focused on self, worship as an event we attend, becomes like a concert or some other forms of entertainment.

As a reaction to this distortion, some reject corporate worship altogether. When people choose to only worship "in private," it is like "throwing the baby out with the bathwater." Just because we have argued over how to reverence the Lord, it doesn't mean corporate worship is at fault. The Bible is clear that worship has a corporate component.

The "worship-in-private" advocates usually ask, "Well, are you saying a person cannot worship on the bank of the river or on a peak in the mountains?" Of course not. That question is irrelevant because God expects worship in both places. It is not an "either-or" choice; it is a "both and" choice. God has designed worship with corporate benefits that cannot be achieved alone. When a whole church worships in unity, the Holy Spirit moves in remarkable ways. There are dynamics of the worship experience that cannot occur without the involvement of others.

Paul exhorted churches, "Let the word of Christ richly dwell within you, with all wisdom teaching and admonishing **one another** with psalms and hymns and spiritual songs, singing with thankfulness in your hearts to God." (Colossians 3:16) "…speaking to **one another** in psalms and hymns and spiritual songs, singing and making melody in your heart to the Lord" (Ephesians 5:19 emphasis mine).

Hebrews 10:25 says, "…not forsaking our own **assembling together**, as is the habit of some, but encouraging one another; and all the more as you see the day drawing near."

As crucial as corporate worship is, it must never be perceived as an event. Worship is a day-by-day lifestyle, and Sunday worship is just another part of that lifestyle. When it is practiced as a lifestyle, it protects us against our tendency to become spectators. Pouring out our praise to God—whether corporate or individual—requires our full personal engagement. If we don't have that, we might as well be attending a concert. After years of prodding people to become worshippers, I finally realized many have never entered the sublime spiritual experience of true worship. **It cannot be explained to someone who has never experienced it.**

A true worshipper is no longer held captive by the attitudes and actions of others. They are free to glorify God in all things, at all times, just as the New Testament describes. "Whether, then, you eat or drink or whatever you do, do all to the glory of God" (1 Corinthians 10:31).

True worship moves us beyond the event mentality into the activity of God daily as we seek to glorify Him in all aspects of life.

2. *Christians have embraced one style as the expression of worship*

When people are asked about their church's form of worship, the answer usually relates to the type of music and musical instruments used, and whether the style of songs is traditional or contemporary. They answer in that way because it's how we typically define worship. I believe the church has tunnel vision when it comes to this subject. Now, let's be honest, we all have our favorite style of devotional music. But, music is only one small piece of true worship. Why then do churches split over this one aspect of the worship experience? In some ways, we are reaping discord because we have sown the seeds of style identity as our concept of how we praise God. When musical style becomes the standard of our identity, we undermine the experiential scope of true worship.

Back in John 4, Jesus told the Samaritan woman, "God is spirit, and those who worship Him must worship in spirit and truth." In this, Jesus revealed God's perspective of worship. He says three things which should have a direct influence on our experience of worship.

First, *God is spirit.* This is a classical definition of the nature of God. Jesus was saying worship is not about a place (the temple in His day) but begins with a personal relationship with the Living God.

Next, He says true worshippers *worship in spirit*. This does not refer to the Holy Spirit, even though worship is empowered by the Holy Spirit. Jesus was saying devotion must be internal and not focused on the external expressions such as rituals, performances, and ceremonies. True worship must be from the heart and does not merely conform to outward religious standards.

Finally, He said we must *worship in truth*. Worship from the heart must be consistent with the truth God has already revealed about Himself in the Scriptures. Jesus was saying that since He (the Messiah) had come, all true worshippers would no longer be identified by where or how they worshipped but by who they worshipped.

Jesus not only became the One we worship, but He also became the example of our worship. Like a tuner on a grand piano, Jesus continually tuned His heart to obey what the Father spoke. He said, "For I did not speak on My own initiative, but as the Father, Himself who sent Me has given me a commandant as to what to say and what to speak. I know that His commandment is eternal life; therefore, the things I speak, I speak just as the Father has told Me" (John 12:49-50).

"...When you lift up the Son of Man, then you will know that I am He, and I do nothing on My own initiative, but I speak these things as the Father taught Me. And He who sent Me is with Me; He has not left Me alone, for I always do the things that are pleasing to Him" (John 8:28-29).

While on this earth, Jesus pleased God in all aspects of His life. So, to enlarge our own concept of worship, here are a few things we can learn from Him:

Jesus worshipped by surrendering to the will of God—Luke 22:42

Jesus worshipped through prayer—Matthew 14:23

Jesus worshipped by serving—John 13:5-9

The church needs to embrace this larger definition of a worshipper. If we do that, Christians will elevate worship to the daily experience God desires for us.

3. Christians have become stagnant attempting to honor their tradition

Tradition is a potent force in the life of a person or a church. The challenge for us in the church is to honor our heritage without becoming bound by it. In far too many cases, the conflicts related to worship are about the age of songs, the familiarity of songs, and the musical arrangement of songs. We have allowed our worship tradition to block anything new. The result is a church culture that is struggling to maintain its relevance in an ever-changing

119

world. I am not saying all worship traditions are wrong. I love great hymns of the faith that declare the character of God, the power of the cross and freedom from sin. But, churches must accept that God continues to inspire powerful new music through modern-day writers and musicians.

Through the centuries God has been inspiring new music for the church. But the word, "new" has almost become a dirty word in the vocabulary of some Christians. So what do we do with the scriptural evidence that God loves new and diverse things:

"I will sing a new song to You, O God." (Psalm 144:9)

"He put a new song in my mouth, a song of praise to our God…" (Psalm 40:3)

"Sing to Him a new song; Play skillfully with a shout of joy." (Psalm 33:3)

"Sing to the Lord a new song; Sing to the Lord all the earth." (Psalm 96:1)

Sing to the Lord a new song, for He has done wonderful things, His right hand and His holy arm have gained the victory for Him." (Psalm 98:1)

"Praise the Lord! Sing to the Lord a new song, and His praise in the congregation of the godly ones." (Psalm 149:1)

Sing to the Lord a new song, Sing praise from the end of the earth!" (Isaiah 42:10)

And they sang a new song, saying, Worthy are You to take the book and to break its seals; for You were slain, and purchased for God with Your blood men from every tribe and tongue and nation." (Revelation. 5:9)

Do you get the idea that God is in favor of new songs that express His glory in worship? To me, there is a glaring contradiction in the argument about traditional songs vs. new songs. That is, **at one point, every traditional song was a new song!** In the history of hymn writing, John and Charles Wesley have few equals. I grew up in the Methodist church, so I am very familiar with these founding fathers of the church. The songs they wrote in the 1700s, which are now considered great hymns of the faith, were openly criticized and rejected by the Church of England. Why? Because the Wesley brothers wrote their songs to the tunes of music popular in the English pubs. Their new songs were intentionally adapted to the style of their culture.

God wants worshippers to love Him with their whole heart. According to Jesus, anything less is hypocrisy! All outward motions of worship are in vain if we behave differently outside the church than we do within it. Jesus gives a wake-up call to all church leaders in his Matthew 15 exchange with the Pharisees about the issue of tradition: Examine what you are doing and why. Never allow tradition to dictate your worship; for when you do, it is no longer about God; it is about you!

4. Christians have created an environment in which worship is about getting

The consumerist mindset we described in a previous chapter extols freedom of choice. But when it comes to worship, the "have it your way" approach is selfish and ultimately destructive. Church leaders who try to serve up a worship style based on "what the customers want" will face constant pressure. They know the patience level of the congregation is low and if they are unhappy some other church may lure them away.

This insidious, intolerant "I want it my way" attitude caused one of the most disappointing and painful times in my ministry career. Our church had to replace a worship leader who was stepping aside after 20 years of service. The new leader wanted to make some changes. I knew this would create tension, but I tried to make it a win-win situation for everyone as we made the transition.

In a congregation of several hundred people, I knew some had hardened positions on traditional versus contemporary worship style. I asked everyone to pray and exercise patience during the transition. I quickly learned that I had significantly overestimated the spiritual maturity level of our church. One element launched a protest, refusing to come into the auditorium until our new worship leader finished leading her set of worship. While waiting in the lobby, they would loudly criticize, judge and undermine what was happening in the service.

Meanwhile, singers who often did solos and special music under the previous worship leader complained their "stage time" was now limited. They set out to undermine the support for me as pastor by making home visits to influential members to voice their displeasure. Lay leaders in key positions began secretly rallying opposition. I wish I had a happy ending to this story. I wish I could say we solved the problem and everyone lived happily ever after, but I can't. The spiritually toxic atmosphere created by all those who wanted their own way crippled the church.

The truth is that we live in a time of such self-absorption that we often hear complaints like "I'm just not getting anything out of the worship service." If you have ever made that statement, consider this: Where is it written that the worship service is for you anyway? If you keep shopping for a church with the right music, style, musicians, personality, and talent to meet your needs, you will have constant frustration. Worship is not designed for us. It is all for God!

A friend told me the story of a couple who decided to leave an evangelical church and go to a traditional liturgical church. The new church had many rituals that were new to the couple. After attending for about three months, the pastor asked them how they were adjusting. The wife responded, "Well, I am doing okay, but there are still times when I don't get anything out of the worship. The pastor responded, "Since when does that matter?" In effect, he was reminding the woman that worship is about giving, not receiving. Churches are imploding due to conflict from self-oriented people who wrongly believe the church exists for them to get rather than for them to give. Scripture tells us what is required of a true worshipper:

"Give unto the Lord the glory due to His name" (Psalm 29:2).

"Ascribe to the Lord the glory due His name; bring an offering and come before Him, worship the Lord in holy array" (1 Chronicles 16:29).

"The sacrifices of God are a broken spirit; a broken and contrite heart, O God, You will not despise" (Psalm 51:17).

In an internet message by Joe McKeever entitled, *Seven Things We Regularly Get Wrong About Worship*, he summarizes the truth about self-centered worship:

"Self-centeredness destroys all worship. If my focus is on myself when I enter the church—getting my needs met, learning something, hearing a lesson that blesses me, being lifted by the singing—then Christ has no part in it. He becomes my servant, and the pastor (and all other so-called performers) is there only for me. It's all about me. We have strayed so far from the biblical concept of worship—giving God His due in all the ways He has commanded—it's a wonder we keep going to church. It is even a greater wonder that our leaders keep trying to get us to worship."

5. Christians have allowed the church to become a stage for fleshly behavior

There is no area of the church the Devil loves to sabotage more than worship. He literally hates it when we worship. So, what does Satan do? He disrupts true worship with all the side-shows he can create. The result is a public display of fleshly behavior in the church as we have never experienced before.

When we see books with titles like, *America's Worship Wars, Beyond the Worship Wars* and *Putting an End to Worship Wars*, it's easy to recognize the impact of this war on Christian worship. The fact that such books have been written indicates a rise of conflict born not of the Spirit, but of the flesh. This "war" is leaving casualties across the church landscape. This grieves my heart, and I know it breaks the heart of God. I am not a guy who sees a demon behind every door, nor do I blame Satan for human weakness. However, when a church allows fleshly behavior to go unchecked, it opens the door to all other kinds of demonic activity.

Proverbs 6 says, "These six things the Lord hates, yes seven are an abomination to Him." At the top of the list is pride. Anytime a pastor, worship leader, musician or speaker draws our attention away from God, and toward themselves, it is an affront to the Lord. Yet how many times have we seen it happen? Pride often manifests in perfectionistic performance orientation, in flashy or suggestive clothing, in self-inflating comments, and at times when speakers become hucksters, doing long sales pitches for things that benefit them personally. A time intended for God's glory displays the very behavior God says He hates. The root of this conflict is identified for us in James 3. Read this Scripture in view of the "worship war" mentality and see what conclusion you reach.

"Who among you is wise and understanding? Let him show by his good behavior his deeds in gentleness of wisdom. But if you have **bitter jealousy** and **selfish ambition** in your heart, do not be arrogant and so lie against the truth. This wisdom is not that which comes down from above but is earthly, natural, demonic. For where **jealousy** and **selfish ambition** exist, there is disorder and every evil thing" (James 3:13-16-emphasis mine).

James paints a sad but accurate picture of what is happening today. Selfish ambition and jealousy are causing havoc by introducing "disorder" and "every evil thing." Our churches must be on guard for any behavior that contradicts the character of Christ.

I want to close this chapter with a reminder from author Charles Swindoll's book, *The Church Awakening*: "You do not need comfortable surroundings or the soft seats of a pew. You don't need a choir or a praise band. You don't need a pipe organ or a drum set. Those elements may assist you, but worship must be part of your daily walk with God...in every part of your personal life. Otherwise, we're just consumers. Or worse, we're opponents in a worship war.

"It's at this point that we need to stop and reconsider what's important—then go there, not only as individuals but as a church. When we do, it quickly becomes obvious that what we are missing is the one essential ingredient without which we cannot grow deeper and reach that satisfying realm for which we were made—worship. God seeks those who will worship Him. Worship focuses on how worthy our God is. Worship is the declaration of His supreme majesty. It is being so preoccupied with the importance of our God that nothing urgent on this earth gains a significant place in our thinking. As this occurs, we discover that there's a dimension to life that is supernatural and unseen...and the invisibility of it only adds to its invincibility."

Personal Inventory

Answer each question based on what is true today in your life. This will point out places you need to adjust your perspective and experience. If unsure, answer what is predominantly true.

1. I believe worship is a lifestyle, not an event.

2. I enjoy and embrace a diversity of expressions in worship style.

3. I believe true worship is more than songs and music.

4. I accept newer contemporary songs with equal value as traditional hymns.

5. I realize my likes and dislikes in worship style are just personal preferences without biblical validation.

6. I understand that discord over worship style is never biblically justifiable.

7. I focus on the posture of my own heart during worship.

8. I am mature enough to honor the worship preferences of others.

9. I believe worship is about "giving to God" rather than personal enjoyment.

10. I can connect with God in worship regardless of the style of music.

Count the number of "yes" answers and number of "no" answers. If you have more "no" answers than "yes" answers, you need to re-evaluate your view of worship as it relates to your church experience.

Chapter 7

DEVALUING OF RELATIONSHIPS

"Every congregation has a choice to be one of two things. You can choose to be a bag of marbles, single units that don't affect each other except in collision. On Sunday morning, you can choose to go to church or to sleep in: Who really cares whether there are 192 or 193 marbles in a bag? Or you can choose to be a bag of grapes. The juices begin to mingle, and there is no way to extricate yourselves if you tried. Each is part of all. Part of the fragrance. Part of the stuff."

Anne Ortlund

Author of *Up With Worship*

Do you remember when you were in elementary school and you were becoming aware of the opposite sex? In fourth grade, I noticed a pretty girl in my class. I wanted to talk to her, but what would I say? Then, the idea came; I'll write her a love note. What girl could resist that? The note was deep with fourth-grade insight. It went something like this; "I like you, do you like me? Please check the box below; yes, no or maybe."

130

We can look back and laugh at those moments now, but they were very real in fourth grade. Why did I fear being rejected, even at such a young age? It was for the same reason then as it is now; we are created by God for relationships!

They are such a priority that God builds everything we will ever learn or experience on the foundation of relationships. It is a two-fold relationship; one is vertical (with God), and one is horizontal (with one another).

While answering a question from the Sadducees about which commandment in the law was the greatest, Jesus said, "You shall love the Lord your God with all your heart, and with all your soul, and with all your mind. This is the great and foremost commandment. The second is like it, you shall love your neighbor as yourself. On these two commandments depend the whole Law and the Prophets" (Matthew 22:37).

The Jews surely were pleased when Jesus affirmed the command in Deuteronomy 6:5 to "love the Lord your God..." But, He rocked their world and changed the entire context of Christianity by making the command to "love your neighbor" of equal importance. To this day we also struggle with His directive to function in loving, biblical relationships. Why? It is easier to love God whom we cannot see than to love difficult people we do see. Relationships are not easy, but they are essential. So much so, that John gave us this alarming warning:

"If someone says, I love God, but hates a Christian brother or sister, that person is a liar; for if we don't love people we can see, how can we say we love God, whom we have not seen? And God Himself has commanded that we must love not only Him but our Christian brothers and sisters, too" (2 John 4:10-20 NLT).

It's quite simple. Love within the church produces unity, and unity draws people to Christ. Relational failures push them away. We have been deceived if we believe we can have a close relationship with God regardless of how we treat each other.

I believe **everything we experience with God is both unreal and unproven until it is lived-out in the context of relationships**. It is easy to be spiritual when we are alone with God, but our spirituality must pass the test of our various relationships. This is the essence of Christianity. We cannot grasp the fullness of the gospel without a commitment to love and serve others.

I love author Anne Ortlund's description of Christians as either marbles or grapes. In her book *Up with Worship* she writes, "The early Christians didn't bounce around like loose marbles, ricocheting in all directions. Picture them as a cluster of ripe grapes, squeezed together by persecution, bleeding and mingling into one another. Fellowship and worship, then, is genuine Christianity freely shared among God's family members. It's sad to think of how many Christians today are missing that kind of closeness. Sermons and songs, while uplifting and necessary, provide only part of a vital church encounter. We need involvement with others too. If we roll in and out of church each week without acquiring a few grape juice stains, we really haven't tasted the sweet wine of fellowship."

God's emphasis on relationships goes even deeper as we consider the many "one another commands" found in the New Testament.

Be at peace with one another—Mark 9:50

Love one another deeply—1 Peter 1:22 (21 times in New Testament)

Be devoted to one another—Romans 12:10

Honor one another—Romans 12:10

Live in harmony with one another—Romans 12:16

Do not judge one another—Romans 14:13

Accept one another—Romans 15:17

Instruct one another—Romans 15:14

Equal concern for one another—1 Corinthians 12:25

Serve one another in love—Galatians 5:13

Carry one another's burdens—Galatians 6:2

Be patient with one another—Ephesians 4:2

Be kind and compassionate to one another—Ephesians 4:32

Forgive one another—Colossians 3:13

Submit to one another—Ephesians 5:21

Honor others before self—Philippians 2:3

Admonish one another—Colossians 3:16

Encourage one another—1 Thessalonians 5:11

Spur one another on to love—Hebrews 10:24

Confess your sins to one another—James 5:16

Pray for one another—James 5:16

Offer hospitality to one another—1 Peter 4:9

Clothe yourself with humility toward one another—1 Peter 5:5

Now, let me be clear; I am not saying that living according to the relational commands of Scripture is easy. At times, I feel like the cartoon character, Garfield (the Cat), when he says, "The world would be a wonderful place if it weren't for people." Regardless of how difficult it is, or how irritated I get, or how unfairly I am treated, I must remember, there are no exceptions to the love your neighbor command.

As the church has become more culturally secularized, so has our behavior toward one another. The lifestyle of Christians is now so far removed from biblical standards that I wonder if the problem is biblical illiteracy or open disobedience. To understand basic biblical behavior, there is practical instruction for us in Romans 12.

First, there is an expression of authentic love for one another.

"Let love be without hypocrisy. Abhor what is evil; cling to what is good. Be devoted to one another in brotherly love; give preference to one another in honor" (Romans 12:9-10).

We use the word "love" so loosely that it no longer carries true meaning. This Scripture challenges us to never be "two-faced" in the way we treat people—acting one way to their face and another way behind their back.

The Scripture is also clear regarding the motivational priority of love. The much-quoted love chapter of 1 Corinthians 13 warns us, "If I speak with the tongues of men and of angels, but do not have love, I have become a noisy gong or a clanging cymbal. If I have the gift of prophecy and know all mysteries and all knowledge; and if I have all faith, so as to remove mountains, but do not have love, I am nothing. And if I give all my possessions to feed the poor, and if I surrender my body to be burned, but do not have love, it profits me nothing."

Right theology is not a substitute for love; religious

works are not a substitute for love; supernatural experience is not a substitute for love; legalistic practices are not a substitute for love, and surrendering all you possess is not a substitute for love.

Second, there is sensitivity as to what others are going through.

"Rejoice with those who rejoice, and weep with those who weep" (Romans 12:15). Christians must willingly walk through life experiences with each other. We need to practice rejoicing in the blessings of others without envy; as well as showing them compassion without judgment during times of hurt. But before we can see the needs of those around us, we must first get our eyes off ourselves.

Third, there is equal acceptance of others.

"Be of the same mind toward one another; do not be haughty in mind, but associate with the lowly. Do not be wise in your own estimation" (Romans 12:16).

There should never be any class warfare in the body of Christ. Anytime you treat someone as less important, you first make yourself of more importance. Jesus calls that pride! There are countless numbers of people no longer attending church because cliques within the church rejected them. This is so opposite the spirit of Jesus. He treated old and young, rich and poor, male and female with equal respect. There is no place for prejudice or self-importance within the life of the church. Both are a contradiction of the gospel and are considered sin in the Scripture.

Fourth, there is self-control between one another.

"Never pay back evil for evil to anyone. Respect what is right in the sight of all men. If possible, so far as it depends on you, be at peace with all men" (Romans 12:17-18).

Like many others, I have been hurt by Christians much more than by non-Christians. Whether it is caused by their unresolved hurts, abrasive personality or differences of opinion, people can be mean. Churches are filled with wounded people who have put protective walls around their heart. Their attempt to insulate themselves against further pain often makes them so closed they cannot be the kind of person God created them to be.

It is impossible to love when you are unwilling to interact whole-heartedly with others. We cannot prevent people from saying or doing hurtful things to us. So, what do we do? We can make a commitment to control our responses to their behavior. Just because someone hurts us, we do not have the right to hit back at them. In the typical church, Christians are devouring one another, justifying hurtful behavior because they suffered first. Look again at what Paul said, "As long as it depends on you..." You are responsible for your reaction.

Fifth, there is an example of righteousness before others.

"Do not be overcome by evil but overcome evil with good" (Romans 12:21). The church should be the place where righteousness reigns. Remember, the earlier conclusion—everything we experience with God is both unreal and unproven until it is lived-out in the context of relationships. Righteousness reigns when those in the church commit to living by God's standard of behavior rather than by feelings or fleshly desires.

You may be thinking at this point, okay, I hear what you're saying, but what's the big deal about relationships in the church? The big deal is that church is all about relationships. The church is not defined by buildings but by the people who occupy those buildings. The health of a church is directly linked to the health of the relationships within it.

The dysfunction of personal relationships within the church is a major contributing factor to the decline of influence the church is experiencing in our culture. But we can change that. The church can once again become a beacon of love and hope if we will embrace the heart of the gospel message.

The high priority of forgiveness

The unity Jesus wants for us will not be achieved unless we practice a lifestyle of forgiveness. The word forgiveness is commonly spoken in the church, but not so commonly practiced. How many church services have you attended which focused on forgiving offenses or traumatic events from the past? Probably not many; if any!

Forgiveness is one of the most essential teachings of Jesus. Countless churches are bound up with dysfunction and disunity because they are filled with people who have never forgiven the hurts in their life. Eventually, they perpetuate the pain by hurting others. Thus, a personal issue becomes a church issue. Sadly, it happens even among pastors.

I know this because for 15 years I had a broken relationship with my ministry mentor (more on this story later). During those years I struggled to trust people. I always felt like I had to guard my heart against being hurt again. As a result, I built an emotional prison for myself. I always thought of myself as open and approachable, but I kept most everyone at arms-length. While I had outward signs of ministry success, inwardly I felt deepening discontent and isolation. I longed for freedom, and I knew I needed to give and receive forgiveness, but I couldn't seem to find my way back to that bridge. People bound with unforgiveness see life through the lens of previous hurts, and they respond by building walls instead of bridges.

I believe unforgiveness is the most damaging issue in the life of a Christian. It becomes a foothold for Satan to operate in many other areas of a person's life. The people I have counseled who struggle with forgiveness issues do not enjoy the prison they have created for themselves. They want to be free. They know they can be free. But they stumble at the thought of forgiving anyone who has hurt them deeply.

Our choice to forgive is a test of authenticity in the church. Think of how many of our communities have experienced church splits. They usually happen when factions within a church hold offenses toward one another, choose to separate relationally rather than forgive. And think of how many times pastors have heard departing factions say, "God is leading us to birth or build up another church." But how can a group of wounded people support a healthy church after leaving a mess of relational damage at their last one?

If we, who have been forgiven much, don't also forgive, we become like the slave in a story Jesus told that's recorded in Matthew 18. The slave, who had been forgiven a huge debt, refused to forgive a man who owed him a much smaller one. Unforgiveness sealed his own bitter fate.

The church of Jesus must become a model of forgiveness to our communities. Whenever a church becomes known more for division and dysfunction than it is for love, the name and the cause of Christ suffer. When we choose to forgive, it is a visible sign of our gratefulness for having been forgiven.

When Paul was writing about godly love, he included a characteristic regarding dealing with offenses. He says in 1 Corinthians 13:5 that love "does not take into account a wrong suffered." This means that we do not keep a ledger with specifics about offenses that we can later use against someone who offended us.

We can't choose to forgive some sins and dismiss others as unforgivable. We are to forgive all sin, just as Jesus did. How is that possible? In the same way, He did. Jesus was always able to separate the person from their sin. His priority was restored relationship. Jesus' concept of forgiveness is always relational. We forgive so relationships can be restored. Jesus went to extreme measures to secure our forgiveness. It was not based on our actions. For we can never do enough good things to earn God's forgiveness.

As Jesus was dying on the cross, He didn't cast blame or feel self-pity. He prayed for those who hurt Him by saying, "Father, forgive them; for they do not know what they are doing" (Luke 23:24). If anyone had the right to be offended, it was Jesus. But He chose to forgive all offenses against Him. That is our example to follow.

Over the years, I have counseled with Christians who have suffered all manner of trauma (rape, child abuse, violence, betrayal, abandonment, fraud, addictions, war, etc.). I would never minimize the impact of these horrors on their lives, but I have observed that for many the pain of their traumatic event becomes a barrier in their life. Talking about those events is so hard they feel hopelessly stuck. By keeping it internalized, they unknowingly give the person or situation which hurt them the authority to control their present and their future.

My friends Bruce and Toni Hebel, founders of "Regenerating Life Ministries," have spent their lives equipping Christians to experience forgiveness for themselves and to help others to experience freedom too. They share a principle in their book *Forgiving Forward*, which is essential to a lifestyle of forgiveness. "We have to come to the place that we accept the fact that the blood of Jesus has covered all sin, including the ones committed against me." For us to expect more payment is to devalue the sacrifice of Christ for the sins of the world. To demand more payment is to tell God that your standards are higher than His.

No other story in the Bible expresses the truth of a forgiving heart like the story of Joseph. His brothers had sold him into slavery and told their father he was dead; he was falsely accused and imprisoned, and he was forgotten in prison by a released inmate. But through a series of events, God elevated him to a place of authority in Egypt. When his family's survival was being threatened by famine, the same brothers who had sold him years earlier came to Egypt for help. Joseph could have exacted revenge by imprisoning, killing or deporting them. Instead, he comforted them.

"...Joseph said to them, do not be afraid, for am I in God's place? As for you, you meant evil against me, but God meant it for good in order to bring about this present result, to preserve many people alive. So, therefore, do not be afraid; I will provide for you and your little ones. So, he comforted them and spoke kindly to them" (Genesis 50: 19-21).

How many of us would have shown such graciousness? Most people operate with the attitude, "If you hurt me, then you have to suffer the consequences." We base our forgiveness on the amount of pain those who hurt us experience. The truth is: the payment for any sin has nothing to do with us. Since all sin is ultimately against God, all payment must be made to God and not to us. Jesus paid the debt on the cross. We are to place all our wounds, hurts, scars and offenses under His blood; it is sufficient! I love this line from the Hebels' book, "Forgiveness costs me, unforgiveness kills me."

Our ministry of reconciliation

When I was in that broken relationship, I convinced myself I had forgiven him, but each silent year brought Carla and me painful memories of holidays and other shared life events with a man now gone from our lives. I knew well what the Scriptures say about forgiveness and reconciliation, but I didn't take that step which is so essential to the life of the church.

When Jesus took our sin upon Himself and reconciled us to God, He also made a way for us to be reconciled to one another. Forgiveness is the first step, but God's higher purpose is to restore relationship with the people who have offended us. And it begins in the house of God. We should be a model of restored relationships, but many Christians feel no responsibility to be reconciled with an offender until that person shows some sign of being deserving. But even when an offender is truly sorry and has suffered for their sin, it is a hard sell to get most Christians to take the first steps of reconciliation.

This became painfully real to me during that conflict with my first mentor in the faith. Pastor Joe Hebel was like a father to Carla and me. When Carla was 16, her mom died and, because her father frequently traveled in his work, the Hebels became her network of family support. When Carla and I met, I was brought into their family circle too. Everything I knew about faith in Christ, church ministry, and spiritual truth at that time came from the model of Joe Hebel.

When I graduated from college, he invited me to be a staff member at our home church. I gratefully accepted and worked alongside him for four years. Then I felt God was calling us to make a change, and I took a ministry position in Irving, Texas. When I broke the news to Pastor Hebel, his sunny disposition turned to ice. He fumed, he argued, he said the move wasn't God's will.

We went ahead with our move to Texas, but when we left, our relationship with him was severed. For the next 15 years, there was no contact of any kind. I was hurt and disillusioned that my ministry mentor would act this way. I didn't know it then, but his anger and disappointment were based on an unspoken expectation that I would assume his position as pastor when he retired and continue his legacy. When I left, it felt to him like a personal betrayal. Since I knew nothing of those expectations, I responded defensively out of my own hurt.

Of all people, two pastors should have been able to find a path to reconciliation, but we each chose a path of silence and isolation. In truth, I wasn't dealing with it at all. The pain never went away, and neither did a sense of conviction that God wanted to restore our relationship. That finally happened when Joe reached out to me to express his regret for the hurt caused by the conflict and years of broken friendship. He was nearing the end of his life, so perhaps it was God's prompt to get his house in order. In any case, Carla and I felt an urgency to meet with him personally, so we drove to his home in Kentucky. The moment I saw him my heart melted. We each asked forgiveness for our part in the broken relationship, tears flowed, and in that place of humility, our friendship was restored. So much so, that when he died after an extended illness, I spoke at his funeral at his request. Thank God for the power and freedom of reconciliation!

The Apostle Paul reminds us that once we were made new in Christ, we were called to be reconcilers, "Therefore, if anyone is in Christ, he is a new creature; the old things have passed away; behold, new things have come. Now all these things are from God, who reconciled us to Himself through Christ and gave us the ministry of reconciliation, namely, that God was in Christ reconciling the world to Himself, not counting their trespasses against them, and He has committed to us the word of reconciliation. Therefore, we are ambassadors for Christ, as though God were making an appeal through us; we beg you on behalf of Christ, be reconciled to God" (2 Corinthians 5:17-20).

Jesus stressed the importance of healing broken relationships when He said, "Therefore if you are presenting your offering at the altar, and there remember that your brother has something against you. Leave your offering there before the altar and go; first, be reconciled to your brother, and then come and present your offering" (Matthew 5:23-24).

The offering in this passage refers to a gift or presentation we are dedicating to God. The term altar refers to a place of dedication, not just a physical location in a building. It carries with it the idea that all our service before God must be from a pure heart. It leaves no room for unforgiveness and broken relationships.

What would happen in the typical church if those who served in the various capacities of the ministry took this teaching of Jesus seriously? There would either be fewer people serving in ministry or a much healthier congregation. I don't know what troubles me more; the number of broken relationships within the church; or the lack of concern about the number of them in the church.

Some of the most difficult people I have ever encountered in pastoral ministry have had a record of divisive behavior in previous churches. Rather than doing the hard work of mending broken relationships, they treat them like dirty diapers, dumping them when things get messy. Most churches are so eager to gain new members; they do not ask questions about a newcomer's previous church experience. But, we should. Why does a church want to embrace members who are running from conflict in other churches? There should be flashing caution lights when this type of growth becomes a pattern. These people are like "carriers" of a disease, and the church is their breeding ground.

The importance of mutual accountability

Mutual accountability helps protect us from taking relational shortcuts in our life. We all need people we trust to objectively speak into our lives and keep us going in the right direction. Even when it becomes uncomfortable; it is essential for our spiritual development.

"Take care, brethren, that there not be in any one of you an evil, unbelieving heart that falls away from the living God. But encourage one another day after day, as long as it is called Today, so that none of you will be hardened by the deceitfulness of sin" (Hebrews 3:12-13).

When choosing an accountability partner, make sure their relationships are functioning well. Now, I am not talking about an absence of conflict. Even healthy relationships experience conflict. But, how do they respond when conflicts arise? What advice will they give when you are hurt? Is reconciliation going to be a top priority?

Pursuit of peace with others

Christianity is not proven when we love those who love us. It is measured by our treatment of those who hurt us. Do we pursue peace with them? That is the standard of

Jesus: "Treat others in the same way you want them to treat you. If you love those who love you, what credit is that to you? For even sinners love those who love them...But love your enemies, and do good, expecting nothing in return; and your reward will be great, and you will be sons of the Most High; for He Himself is kind to ungrateful and evil men. Be merciful, just as your Father is merciful" (Luke 6:31-32, 35-36).

Can you imagine the radical effect in the typical church if the members committed themselves to be peacemakers? By the way, Jesus said in the Sermon on the Mount in Matthew 5:9, "Blessed are the peacemakers for they shall be called the sons of God." Becoming a peacemaker requires us to make some adjustments in the way we deal with relational conflict. We can no longer walk around the church as a spiritual vigilante—seeking our own form of justice.

As it says in Romans 12, "Never take your own revenge, beloved, but leave room for the wrath of God, for it is written, Vengeance is mine, I will repay, says the Lord. But if your enemy is hungry, feed him, and if he is thirsty, give him a drink; for in so doing you will heap burning coals on his head. Do not be overcome by evil, but overcome evil with good."

The kingdom of darkness has no answer for love and mercy. When we treat people with God's love and mercy, regardless of their treatment of us, it nullifies any agenda they may have. I have seen this happen in the church many times. When people were undermining the ministry behind my back or behaving in a two-faced manner, it was almost humorous to observe their discomfort when I continued to respond to them in love, grace, and mercy. We must believe that God is big enough to handle the situation; we cannot get in God's way and assume His position as judge.

As I close this chapter on relationships, let me repeat the principle that I stated at the beginning. **"Everything we experience with God is both unreal and unproven until it is lived out in the context of relationships."**

Several years ago, I became concerned that our church had become a collection of several hundred disconnected people. For us to function healthily, the congregation needed to grasp this reality too. To create a visual illustration, our staff planned a Sunday service designed to get this point across.

On the designated Sunday (unknown to the congregation) as people entered the auditorium, we had covered tables across the back of the room. Those tables were filled with donuts, pastries, milk, juice, and coffee. Midway into the service, I explained my concern about being disconnected. I said it was difficult to be connected when we didn't even know one another's names. As an illustration, I had everyone stand and talk to the person in front of them, behind them and on each side. After a few minutes, everyone returned to their seat. I then asked, "If you just talked to someone you did not know before today, please stand. It was an incredible sight! Over 95% of the congregation rose to their feet.

I explained the effect of being disconnected and told them they were going to connect as the church today! I instructed them to "fill out a name tag and go eat, drink and meet people you don't know." That may sound like sacrilege to some people, but the impact on our church was immeasurable. It created an awareness of our need for relationship that a sermon would never have accomplished.

It's easy to talk about the value of relationships, but to pursue them and celebrate their value takes effort. Yet it is one of the most biblical and spiritual things we can do!

Personal Inventory

Answer each question based on what is true today in your life. This will point out places you need to adjust your perspective and experience. If unsure, answer what is predominantly true.

1. I believe my relationship with God and with others are of equal importance.

2. I believe the church is defined by relationships.

3. I accept that Christianity can only function in the context of relationships.

4. I agree that I am held accountable by God for how I function with others.

5. I place a high priority on my relationships with others.

6. I am quick to forgive offenses and reconciliation is important to me.

7. I believe I am expected to treat others the same way Christ has treated me.

8. I actively help our church become a safe and accepting place for all people.

9. I personally seek to be a "peacemaker" by being available to resolve conflicts when they arise.

10. I believe people are influenced for or against the gospel by the way we treat one another.

Count the number of "yes" answers and number of "no" answers. If you have more "no" answers than "yes" answers, you need to re-evaluate your view of relationships as it relates to your church experience.

Chapter 8

LACK OF SPIRITUAL UNITY

"Has it ever occurred to you that one hundred pianos all tuned to the same fork are automatically tuned to each other? They are of one accord by being tuned, not to each other, but to another standard to which each one must individually bow. So one hundred worshippers (meeting) together, each one looking to Christ, are in heart nearer to each other than they could possibly be, were they to become "unity" conscious and turn their eyes away from God to strive for closer fellowship."

A.W. Tozer

In the early stage of my ministry, I was part of a church which taught me unity with others outside our denomination was a dangerous thing. We had strict standards of behavior and doctrinal adherence. We could not embrace relationships with those with "different standards," even in ministry associations. There was great fear that the purity of our group would somehow be contaminated by associating with those who were "not of us." Any effort toward unity with people of other denominations was considered as a step toward ecumenicalism.

153

Thankfully, as I matured in biblical understanding and ministry experience, I moved beyond that sphere of influence. As my theological transition was occurring, I had the opportunity to speak at a church whose pastor had been a friend for several years. Even though we now had differences on issues upon which we once agreed, we maintained our relationship. During a visit with his family after a day of church services, I asked about other churches, curious to know what was taking place in their community for the Kingdom. During his answer, my friend's 10-year-old son made a statement I will never forget. He said, "Daddy, they say they are Christians, but I don't think they are our kind of Christians."

Wow! At that moment, every message I had ever preached flashed before my eyes. How many 10-year-olds had I influenced by erroneous teaching? I realized on that day just how much damage is caused by our lack of understanding on spiritual oneness. Coincidentally, that was the last time I ever spoke at his church. I have often wondered if they concluded, I wasn't their kind of Christian either.

My ministry experience is illustrated so accurately by Emo Phillips in a story voted "the funniest religious joke ever" in an online poll in 2005.

Once I saw this guy on a bridge about to jump. I said, "Don't do it!"

He said, "Nobody loves me."

I said, *"God loves you. Do you believe in God?"*

He said, *"Yes."*

I said, *"Are you a Christian or a Jew."*

He said, *"A Christian."*

I said, *"Me too! Protestant or Catholic?"*

He said, *"Protestant."*

I said, *"Me too! What franchise?"*

He said, *"Baptist."*

I said, *"Me too! Northern Conservative Baptist or Northern Liberal Baptist?"*

He said, *"Northern Conservative Baptist."*

I said, *"Me too! Northern Conservative Baptist Great Lakes Region or Northern Conservative Baptist Eastern Region."*

He said, *"Northern Conservative Baptist Great Lakes Region."*

I said, *"Me too! Northern Conservative Baptist Great Lakes Region Council of 1879 or Northern Conservative Baptist Great Lakes Region Council of 1912?"*

He said, *"Northern Conservative Baptist Great Lakes Region Council of 1912."*

I said, *"Die heretic! And I pushed him over."*

Because we've seen this fractious attitude in religious people, this story brings a smile to our faces. But, it is no joke that the world sees the church as such a narrow-minded, disunified body. If the authenticity of Christianity and the practical expression of the church is going to regain its place of influence in our culture, it must begin with God's priority of spiritual oneness.

Jesus focused on this very subject in an encounter with his disciples. "John answered and said, master, we saw someone casting out demons in Your name; and we tried to prevent him because he does not follow along with us. But Jesus said to him; do not hinder him; for he who is not against you is for you" (Luke 9:49-50).

Doesn't it sound like the disciples have just attended the latest denominational meeting? I can almost hear the self-congratulating glee in John's voice when he told Jesus of their encounter. Imagine his surprise when Jesus rebuked him instead of complimenting him! The disciples saw this man "who was not of their group" using methods they considered to be their exclusive domain. Jesus commanded them not to hinder Kingdom work. How many works of God have been thwarted by people who thought they were pleasing God by resisting them. We must keep in mind what Jesus did. Even if a ministry looks different than ours, if the central message is the same, be supportive.

The Body of Christ is being divided by the same attitude in our culture. We are guilty of hindering, avoiding or severing connections with people over things that are eternally trivial. So many in churches today have a faulty understanding of oneness with those beyond our own congregation. They somehow think unity is the same as uniformity (everyone believing and behaving the same way). They even confuse it with conformity (complying with an accepted standard or religious code). Both ideas are distortions of biblical unity.

The biblical definition of unity is "oneness and harmony amid diversity." It carries with it the picture of instruments in an orchestra. Each instrument is unique and is placed in the orchestra for a specific sound. When each plays in harmony with each other, beautiful music is generated. That is the idea of the church. Each person operating in harmony with one another as each person fulfills their specific role.

It's incongruous to think of an orchestra all using just one type of instrument. But isn't that what we do when we want our church to only accept "our kind of people?" One of the world-shaking things about the First Century church was its inclusiveness. It brought together rich and poor, Jew and Gentile, men and women and valued all as equal before God.

God could have created us all exactly alike. Same size, shape, color, intellect, etc. But He didn't. He delights in diversity. I believe a healthy church should be a beautiful blend of the Lord's handiwork. Young and old, rich and poor, families and singles, and people of different races and life experiences.

John 17, Jesus' great prayer for unity of the church that would follow Him, reveals a global purpose for oneness in the faith. "I have given them the glory you have gave Me, so that they may be one, as We are, I in them and You in Me, all being perfected into one. Then the world will know that you sent Me and will understand that You love them as much as You love Me. Father, I want these whom You've given Me to be with Me so they can see My glory. You gave Me the glory because You loved me even before the world began! O Righteous Father, the world doesn't know you, but I do; and these disciples know you sent Me. And I have revealed You to them and will keep on revealing You. I will do this so that Your love for Me may be in them and I in them" (John 17:22-26 NLT).

Jesus uses the oneness that exists between Himself as the Son and God the Father as the standard for oneness in our relationships. Now, I am not suggesting we can have the same level of relationship as the members of the Godhead. But Jesus is indicating through His prayer that believers can experience intimate friendship with God. Even though the Son and the Father are distinct individuals; they are one in spirit, in mission, in purpose, in love. So, Jesus makes the comparison; even though we as Christians are distinct individuals, we are to have one heart and one love "so that the world may know."

A good test of a church's oneness is in whether its prayers center on individual requests or on corporate vision centered on His will. We would do well to ask, *"If God answered all of the prayers that you have consistently prayed, would it change* **your** *world or* **the** *world?"*

Paul challenged the Philippian believers to "... make my joy complete by being of the **same mind**, maintaining the **same love**, united in **one spirit**, intent on **one purpose**. Do nothing from selfishness or empty conceit, but with humility of mind regard one another as more important than yourselves; do not merely look out for your own interests, but also for the interests of others. Have this **attitude in yourselves which was also in Christ Jesus**" (Philippians 2:1-5 emphasis mine).

When the church begins to experience unity, it demonstrates a commitment to God's outward purpose. One of the most beautiful experiences of unity I have encountered occurred several years ago when my church planned a 72-hour prayer event. People were encouraged to participate in one-hour increments throughout the day and night. Corporate worship and prayer were held each evening. This experience of personal repentance, worship and intercession opened the door for an unprecedented spirit of unity. Praying together gave people a clearer view of God's character, as they invested in a cause higher than personal fulfillment. The oneness we experienced in those three days paved the way for God to expand the church's ministry impact long after the prayer event ended.

Oneness is spiritual, not institutional.

When Jesus prayed for us to be one, He no doubt

foresaw the church He was birthing, a body that would extend to every nation. A distortion of this part of His prayer has led many into a legalistic philosophy that requires everyone to look the same, behave the same, think the same and believe the same. Jesus is praying for the individuals within the church, not institutional uniformity. His prayer carries with it the idea that every believer experiences oneness with Christ in the Spirit and in so doing is empowered by the Spirit to practice unity with one another. Consider again the words Jesus uses in His prayer: "That they may be also in Us … I in them and You in Me… I in them." Blended beautifully into the foundation of all unity!

Oneness is visible to those in the world.

In Jesus' prayer, He says that our unity with Christ and with one another must be visible to those around us. Look at verse 23, "*so that the world may know that You sent Me.*" The context of Jesus' prayer is significant. It challenges us with this thought, "How will the world know, understand and believe in God if the unity among Christians is not visible?"

We ought to look and act like the people we profess to be in our songs and prayers: saved, set free, bonded in love, letting our lives bring glory to God. If we profess to believe the gospel has united us is there evidence in our relationships? Embodied in the gospel is a commitment to reconciliation, an openness to relationship with those "different ones" in the body of Christ. The gospel removes barriers between all kinds of people. The power of every barrier between people came crashing down when the veil was torn in two during the crucifixion.

Jesus said, "A new commandment I give to you, that you love one another, even as I have loved you, that you also love one another. By this all men will know you are My disciples, if you have love for one another" (John 13:34-35). We are to live in such love and oneness that the world will have to rethink their convictions about God, Christ, and the church. Our love will convince them Jesus is real.

Another important step toward spiritual oneness is to remove destructive distinctions among believers.

The destructive effect of favoritism

"I charge you, in the sight of God and Christ Jesus and the elect angels, to keep these instructions without partiality, and to do nothing out of favoritism" (1 Timothy 5:21).

Favoritism has been a problem in the church from its very beginning. Paul rebuked church leaders who gave preferential treatment to rich people over poor people. He called it for what it is—sin.

Favoritism is preferential treatment of one person (call it discrimination) on conditions such as race, social class, finances, appearance, abilities, behavior, etc. It shows up in situations like when a pastor's daughter is the only one asked to do choir solos; when special honors are given to big donors, when only white males are ever asked to pray at a church meeting, when elders are chosen based on business success rather than devotion to God, or when other leadership choices are based more on loyalty than faithfulness.

The Bible is clear that favoritism in the church is wrong. Paul declares to both the Romans and Ephesians "... there is no partiality with God." Jesus paid an equal price for every person.

It is difficult to avoid becoming a participant in favoritism. We are drawn to want to work with those we most easily connect with—your family and close friends. But favoritism often goes beyond that. Married people often are shown preference over singles; men over women; loyal members over newcomers, those with special abilities over the disabled.

Even Christ's closest followers struggled with a bias against people who were different from them. When the apostle Peter was first called to minister to non-Jewish people, he was reluctant. He later admitted, "I now realize how true it is that God does not show favoritism, but accepts men from every nation who fear him and do what is right" (Acts 10: 34-35).

The fact that Peter specifically addresses the sin of favoritism implies this was a common problem in the early church. Favoritism and partiality are not from God, regardless of the circumstances. We must work harder to root out this destructive influence. The Lord has called us to love and accept one another just as He did with us—unconditionally. In His eyes, we all are equal.

Relinquishing the right to be right

Another step in the pursuit of spiritual oneness requires people to yield their need to always be right. Every church has them; they turn every discussion into a win-lose proposition. They must be right in every situation and on any issue. They are like the old saying, "They would argue with a fence post."

There was a time in my life when I had to always be right. Okay, there are probably occasions when my wife would say, that need still exists. But there was a time when it was a tremendous weakness in my life. When another person had what I considered to be a *wrong* opinion, I made it my mission to change their view. It bothered me if I couldn't persuade them. Even though I still take the bait and argue from time to time, it's no longer so important to me to influence others to change their minds that I am willing to fight and be divisive.

Some people argue out of habit. But I wonder if it isn't often a result of something much deeper—the sin of pride. Perhaps that's what drove me to be right. It wasn't about the issue; it was about winning and control. There was a piece of my pride at stake in the argument. If I lost, I felt diminished.

As I've grown older, I've found it easier to let things go. If someone makes a provocative statement, I no longer consider it an invitation to a fight. I ask myself, "Will the relationship be helped by an argument?" And if the answer is yes, I ask, "Do I have the energy for it?" The answer to both questions is almost always *no*. A good honest debate is one thing, but arguments fray the fabric of relationships too easily.

For a man who seemed to engage in a lot of arguments, the apostle Paul warned of the danger of being divisive. He said, "Warn a divisive person once and then warn them a second time. After that, have nothing to do with them" (Titus 3:10).

The legacy of a person who must be right is a sad one. The person who prioritizes being right over relationships usually experiences a trail of broken and unreconciled relationships in their life which is a testimony to what drives them. How many church conflicts can be traced back to people allowing pride to drive them to do things or say things they previously never thought possible. Pride is always destructive; it is the root of all divisive behavior. So, what does God say about pride?

He hates it! *"... Pride and arrogance and the way of evil and perverted speech I hate" (Proverbs 8:13). The Bible says* God humbles the proud. When pride enters an area of our heart, He will not leave it untouched. He will discipline us because He loves us too much to allow pride to continue splitting apart people He loves. The path of humility helps us all learn He is God and we are not. It is the way the church learns how to resist divisiveness and experience true oneness.

Some ways to move toward spiritual unity

This journey requires congregations to embrace a broader vision of what we can be corporately and a willingness to make necessary changes. There is no magic formula, but the biblical principles listed below can guide a church in their own journey.

Make a commitment to spiritual truth – Invite God to speak through the Bible, which will transform your thoughts and help you see other believers from His perspective. Regularly read, study, and meditate on His Word, and attend a church where you can hear God's Word taught and applied.

Surrender to the authority of the Holy Spirit – Understand that God stands ready to empower all believers with the Holy Spirit regardless of denomination or affiliation. Know that it's the Spirit's power that will enable you to live the Christian life and experience peace with others.

Use spiritual gifts to encourage and serve others – Realize that every believer has a unique and valuable contribution to make to the Body of Christ. Ask God to help you recognize and develop the spiritual gifts He wants you to use together with other believers to do His Kingdom work.

Overcome evil with good – Come in the opposite spirit against evil in all its forms. Respond to hate with love, to greed with generosity, to gossip with truth, to meanness with kindness, to hopelessness with hope. Pray for the Holy Spirit to help you discern what's going on spiritually in any situation. Be aware that Satan wants to divide; resist his efforts to distance believers from each other.

Seek to please God instead of other people – Be careful about a pre-occupation to be accepted and approved of by people. Don't spend your time and energy trying to earn validation by meeting expectations imposed on you by other people, even if they are fellow believers. Instead, focus on pleasing God through your thoughts, words, and actions.

Pray for each other – Pray regularly for other believers. Get to know them and pray for their specific concerns. Share your concerns with them and ask them to pray for you, as well. It is difficult for division to exist when believers are committed to praying for each other.

Control your thoughts and words – Be proactive about choosing not to think negative thoughts or speak harsh words, which can bring great destruction to your relationships. Ask the Holy Spirit to renew your mind, and help you think positive thoughts and speak encouraging words. Allow the Holy Spirit to be a filter over your tongue; just because you can say something doesn't mean you should.

Jesus makes it unmistakably clear that unity and spiritual oneness reflect the heart and character of God. It is the Spirit of the Kingdom of God. When those in the world want to know what the Kingdom of God is like, we should be able to say, "come to my church and you will see it."

Personal Inventory

Answer each question based on what is true today in your life. This will point out places you need to adjust your perspective and experience. If unsure, answer what is predominantly true.

1. I believe biblical unity is a priority for Christians.

2. I believe unity is more than externals; it is spiritual in nature.

3. I agree that unity (oneness) is possible amid diversity.

4. I agree that unity is based on the same oneness that Jesus and His Father enjoyed.

5. I believe–unity is how the world recognizes we are followers of God.

6. I accept people of all religious backgrounds regardless of differences.

7. I believe we become more unified with others as we experience oneness with Christ.

8. I do believe there is more in the gospel that unites us than divides us.

9. I agree that favoritism and partiality is a sin.

10. I personally try in my church to treat all people with equal value.

Count the number of "yes" answers and number of "no" answers. If you have more "no" answers than "yes" answers, you need to re-evaluate your view of spiritual unity as it relates to your church experience.

CONCLUSION

I have reached an age in life where I look at things more closely in terms of spiritual value. I want to invest my life into things which matter. I feel blessed with the family life and ministry I've had, but I often wonder how much time I have wasted on things with no Kingdom value. I know this is a concern shared by many Christians.

I was mentored earlier in my ministry by the late Leonard Ravenhill, an English-born revivalist, and teacher. He had a sign in his office that read, "Lord, keep me eternity conscious." What a great statement and prayer for all of us. What would happen if we lived each day with those words in the forefront of our mind? How would it change our attitude and actions? Would our words be adjusted? Would our priorities shift? Would we treat others differently? How would the lives of people be changed if the church modeled the life of the Kingdom?

I believe it is time to take an honest look at whether our behavior authenticates what we say we believe.

- If we say God is our top priority, cultivate an ever-deeper relationship through worship and prayer.

- If we say we believe in grace, extend grace to those who disagree.

- If we say we believe in the authority of Scripture, don't behave in contradiction to its commands.

- If we say, we love people, model love in the way we value, accept and treat them.

- If we say we believe in the salvation of people's souls, live in such a way that Christ is exalted before the lost.

- If we say we believe in missions, spend resources on those outside the church rather than on the things in the church or for our personal benefit.

I pray this book will reawaken a longing in your heart to experience the power and passion of authentic Christian life, committing yourself to the things which pass the test of eternity. The choice is yours. What kind of future are you investing in?

Join me in the everyday journey of authentic Christianity!

REFERENCES

Charles Swindoll, *Dropping Your Guard*, (Word Books, 1984) Page 157

Richard Sterns, *The Hole in Our Gospel* (Thomas Nelson, 2009, 10) Page 185

David Platt, *Radical*, (Multnomah Books, 2010) Page 16

Richard Sterns, *The Hole in Our Gospel* (Thomas Nelson, 2009, 10) Pages 179-180

Rubel Shelly, *I Knew Jesus Before He Was a Christian...and Liked Him Better Then*

(Leafwood Publishers, 2011) Page 190

Gordon McDonald, *Strange Things, Strange People, Strange Places: The Unorthodox Ministry of Jesus* (Discipleship Journal, 1991) Pages 32-34

Rubel Shelly, *I Knew Jesus Before He Was a Christian...and Liked Him Better Then*

(Leafwood Publishers, 2011) Page 187

George Barna, *Revolution* (Tyndale House Publishers, 2005) Pages 31-35

Charles Paul Conn, *Making It Happen* (Fleming H. Revell Co., 1981) Page 95

Dallas Willard, *The Spirit of the Disciplines*, quoted in R.J. Foster and J.B. Smith, *Devotional Classics* (San Francisco: HarperOne, 2005) Page 14

John A. Phillips quoted Dietrich Bonhoeffer in, *The Form of Christ in the World: A Study of Bonhoeffer's Christology* (London: Collins, 1967) Page 100

William Barclay, *The Gospel of Luke* (Westminster Press, 1975) Page 595.

Neil T. Anderson and Robert L. Saucy, *The Common Made Holy* (Harvest House Publishers, 1997) Page 109

Chuck Gaines, *10 Questions for Formulating a Discipleship Process* (LifeWay Publishing, 2009)

Anne Ortlund, *Up with Worship* (Regal Books, 1975)

JR Woodward, *A Working Definition of Success* (JR Woodward Blog Post, 2006)

Theodore Roosevelt, *Citizenship in a Republic* (Speech delivered in Paris, 1910)

Charles Hummel, *The Tyranny of the Urgent* (InterVarsity Christian Fellowship, 1967) Pages 4-5

Gordon Dahl, *Work, Play and Worship in a Leisure-Oriented Society* (Minneapolis: Augsburg, 1972) Page 12

Charles Swindoll, *The Church Awakening* (FaithWords, 2010) Pages 116, 142

Bruce and Toni Hebel, *Forgiving Forward* (Regenerating Life Press, 2011) Page 87

Rubel Shelly, *I Knew Jesus Before He Was a Christian...and Liked Him Better Then*

(Leafwood Publishers, 2011) Page 10

A.W. Tozer, *The Pursuit of God* (Harrisburg: Christian Publications, 1948)

ABOUT THE AUTHOR

John Offutt is a speaker, certified life coach and pastor. He has been in pastoral ministry since 1974. He serves as the teaching pastor at LifeSource Community Church in Lindale, Texas. He also leads John Offutt Ministries, a ministry committed to revitalizing authenticity within the Body of Christ. He and his wife Carla have been married for 46 years and have 3 married daughters and 8 grandchildren.

MINISTRY INFORMATION

For information on how to schedule a speaking engagement, conference or Life Coaching session, please log onto: JohnOffutt.com

John Offutt Ministries
PO Box 517
Lindale, TX 75771

Follow us on Facebook @ John Offutt or through our blog @ JohnOffutt.com